PEOPLE'S IDENTITY

RACE AND RACISM

SIMON LENNON

People's Identity: Race and Racism
Non-fiction
Race Relations, Ethnic Studies
A book in the collection: The West
A book in the series: Identity
Published by Pine Hill Books
Copyright © 2015, 2021 Simon Lennon.
ISBN 978-1-925446-00-5 (electronic)
ISBN 978-1-925446-14-2 (paperback)
59,000 words, plus bibliography, references to 65,000 words
Cover image: Sydney Opera House concert hall, 2013

In memory of my old Irish grandmother

CONTENTS

1. RACISM

We in the West identify with the world. The world doesn't identify with us.

The world doesn't identify with anyone or everyone. Among the students studying for a Master of Business Administration degree with me was a toothpaste company executive, Lenore. As part of a group project in 1995, we investigated the Colgate-Palmolive company's marketing of dental hygiene products in Papua New Guinea, a parliamentary democracy within the British Commonwealth, with the British monarch the head of state. The Western company executives and marketers assumed that people the world over would relate to the company's film of children from all manner of races cleaning their teeth. Perhaps the white-skinned expatriates living behind barbed wire in Port Moresby compounds did.

Papua New Guineans didn't. They weren't part of the racial polyglot presented before them, part of that world. That was America. They were Melanesian.

Traditional tribalism remains important to Melanesians and many other races, but race is and will remain the primary human identity. Other races retaining their racial identities mightn't necessarily mean white people should revive ours. It does make me wonder why not.

Race makes identity easy. In 1948, between his two terms as Australian prime minister, Sir Robert Menzies proudly declared himself "British to his bootstraps." Australians were British, as Australian law denoted until 1949. Being Australian was our point of distinction with other British, like New Zealanders and Canadians (but not Quebecois French). To the rest of the world, we were one in the same. We didn't cease being British for being away from our Isles a few hundred years.

We might have been more particularly Irish, Scottish, or Welsh, which could matter aside the dominant English. My mother's mother was proudly a Burke, who called herself my "old Irish grandmother." She never left Australia in her life.

Our races gave us hearts, histories, and heroes. They made each of us someone; we knew who we were. My parents spoke proudly of seeing maps of the earth where the red denoting the British Empire covered so many countries: the empire on which the sun never set. We were peoples with cultures and futures for which to prepare.

We were nations between each other, but bracketed ourselves to be European when we encountered non-Europeans. Merged into our pan-European identity, we were white.

That became most acute after World War II. Britain's Prime Minister Winston Churchill (who'd pitted Britons against Germans before it again became fashionable) was among those craving that we embrace our collective European identity to avert further war. Remaining a British nationalist, Churchill didn't imagine us surrendering our national selves, but we did in time surrender.

In Australia, we accepted waves of immigrants from Continental Europe. My father called them New Australians, until the term became discriminatory and discrimination for the West became wrong. We became Anglo-Celts; never before had the English been so muddled with the Irish. A pan-European status came to being Australian, but even our pan-European West became impractical with waves of immigrants from outside. When we ceased identifying with our race, we lost our identity.

The sun set on our empires. It set by our hands.

There'd come a new word: racism. Initially, it meant white people's malice to other races. It came quickly to mean our prejudice against them, and then believing race had practical consequences. Soon enough, it meant us remembering race.

Wherever European peoples live in the world, we'd stopped identifying with our living and our dead. Race we now find confronting.

When he was six years old, in 2002, my eldest son played soccer. Each Saturday morning, parents of the ten boys in his team watched their sons rush around the field, as much after the rest of the pack as after the ball. We applauded the rare goals either team scored, hoping our sons improved a little each week. We weren't altogether sure that they did.

Amidst the conversations during one game, a parent wanted to remark about a talented player from the opposing team. Not knowing his name, or indeed the names of any players from opposing teams, she tried to identify him by his movements: his place to the side of most other boys. If his jersey carried a number she couldn't see it. When that description was unclear, she tried describing him by his skills: his hurried turn. That also failed, so she reluctantly mentioned his size: he was smaller than other boys on the field.

She never mentioned his race. He was the only Chinese, the only Asian.

The freedoms we had to be British, Australian, American and so forth, we no longer have. We don't even know what they mean. I'm not sure I do.

I think it was late in the first decade of the new millennium that a British newspaper (*The Sun*, I think) asked its readers to say what they thought it meant to be British. Among the many detailed replies, one was conspicuously brief. In just a handful of words, the reader said being British meant carrying a British passport. That was all, nothing more, nothing less.

Other readers made longer-winded expressions of much the same idea, or spoke of a slightly more exacting definition requiring British citizenship. It seemed very little.

Their definitions made British the people who'd waged war against Britain, if they took a British passport that morning. They excluded people who'd defended our fighting Isles, and whose ancestors died doing so, but whom that morning surrendered British citizenship to join her former colonies.

To say our identity lies in the passport we hold, citizenship, or other documentation, is to say we have no identity. Li Cunxin could be known the world over as the last dancer to Chinese leader Mao Zedong, defect to America, move to Australia in 1995, and fourteen years later be named Australian Father of the Year. In the words of the *Sydney Morning Herald* newspaper, he wasn't just an Aussie dad. He was the "*top Aussie dad.*"

Through my several visits to America in the 1990s, I was often bemused to hear Americans call their country the home of the free. When I wasn't bemused. I could be annoyed. Mike, a Washington lawyer, was the only American with whom I had the chance to point out that other countries are also free. I didn't proceed to say it, but being a land of liberty isn't a definition of any one country when others enjoy liberty too. However fine might be their freedoms, they aren't uniquely America's.

Addressing the American University School of International Service in Washington the first day of July 2011, President Barack Obama said being American "is not a matter of blood or birth." He didn't say what being American is.

His vice president Joe Biden did, addressing the United States Hispanic Chamber of Commerce's 2014 Legislative Summit and citing President Theodore Roosevelt's speech titled 'True Americanism' in 1894. "Americanism is not a question of birthplace or creed or a line of descent. It's a question of principles, idealism, and character."

Roosevelt spoke at a time America restricted immigration by race. His America was a North European melting pot. (Southern Europe's melting pots were in Latin America; Argentinians, Chileans, and Uruguayans were distinctions from other Spaniards, otherwise one in the same.) America's immigrants Anglicised their names leaving no observable distinction with other Americans; they Americanised them.

By the time of Biden, only the idealism remained, but it's no longer the immigrants'. It's ours. Biden believed illegal immigrants were already American.

Never to be outdone by Americans, Australia's Department of Immigration and Citizenship issued its Australian Values Statement in 2007. Applicants for immigration needed to sit a multiple-choice examination, ticking boxes on a government questionnaire supposedly ensuring they respected the freedom and dignity of the individual, equality of men and women, freedom of religion, commitment to the rule of law, a spirit of egalitarianism that embraced mutual respect, tolerance, fair play, compassion for those in need in pursuit of the public good, and equal opportunity for individuals, regardless of their race, religion, or ethnicity. (They could've been the stated values of almost any country on earth, including those that discriminate by race or religion.)

In 2007, Prime Minister Gordon Brown thought values were the only way to define being British in the era of multiple races. A complicated process of submissions and consultations, including a summit of up to a thousand citizens, would determine those values. The *Times* newspaper responded with a competition to choose a new motto for the country. A fifth of respondents chose *"No Motto Please, We're British."*

The need to define who we are is a peculiarly postmodern quest for the West. Few countries elsewhere imagine it.

In 2009, President Nicholas Sarkozy (the son of a Hungarian aristocrat and a French Jewess, with a little more in her besides) proposed a debate about what it meant to be French. Alain Juppe was one of several former prime ministers who objected, believing such a debate would stigmatise immigrants. For Juppe, being French was what it had been since the French Revolution: liberty, equality, and fraternity. He was idealistic and thus ideological, implying the first Frenchmen were the 1789 revolutionaries. Frenchmen or women not sharing those values weren't French. Other people on earth believing them presumably were.

Juppe's definition excluded immigrants he presumed to include. "Liberty, egalitarianism, and fraternity are not shared values," a young black Muslim in Marseilles told American Jewish film-maker Ami Horowitz early in 2015, after three Muslims massacred seventeen people at the *Charlie Hebdo* magazine offices and a kosher supermarket in Paris. "On freedom of expression, there is a conflict."

Our vision of a single world people makes ideals our identity, but any identity based upon values has to be vague. Hardly a country anywhere doesn't claim liberty, equality, and fraternity, interpreting each as it chooses. One person's liberty is another person's constraint. Equality of opportunity is at odds with equality of outcome; people aren't equal. Fraternity presupposes something joining us, with no suggestion of what that could be. Whenever we try to define ourselves with values, they become more words we bandy about, without thought as to how free we are.

If we think words define us, then we're undefined. Identities depending on words aren't identities. They're words. We fail to define, and so fail to comprehend ourselves or anyone else.

Whatever Sarkozy imagined, nothing came of it. A little more than a year later, at the end of 2010 in his annual address to the people of France, he defended his country's use of the beleaguered euro currency by saying Europe was "essential to our future, to our identity, and to our values."

Europe is no longer racial. It's money.

Our values mightn't be much, but they're all that we have, along with our currencies. If there's identity in values, it's the identity shared throughout our postmodern West: a conglomerate Western identity masquerading as national identities we all have in common. Rights and self-righteousness define no country, but the West's rejection of racism, not all racism but only our racism, defines us all. It's our identity no less surely than race used to be. None of our other values, minor identities, or anything else, not even us, matter as much. It's our certainty, conviction, and existential sense of what we are.

White people can preach all we like about uniting different races with common values. For growing numbers of people, that's more of our white privilege: expecting other races to ignore race because we do.

I know little of other races, as they know little of us, but they enjoy no end of clubs, coalitions, and countries predicated upon race. I learnt of American Indians in Film and Television, the Black Media Alliance, the National Hispanic Media Coalition, and the Korean American Bar Association in 2012, when their representatives turned up at the Los Angeles City Council to condemn racism on Los Angeles radio (but not racism in the formation of their associations and alliances).

In their best respects, we of the West could pause and examine other races' attitudes to themselves and others in contrast to our attitudes to ours. While we made racial blindness a virtue, other races aren't so virtuous. They don't deny what they see, but we can't see it because we see only individuals. They remain defined by their race without thought of being anything else, retaining their racial roots.

For a while there, we rationalised our rejection of only white racism by saying minority races needed redress from powerful majorities. If that were really our only consideration, we'd have not let them immigrate from where they'd been majorities and they'd not have come, except to empower minorities already here.

Minorities rule suits minorities better than majorities, but becoming minorities in streets, suburbs, and whole cities hasn't allowed us to enjoy our racial identities. We still refuse to form business, cultural, sporting, or other associations around race. We condemn any of us who do. Matthew Heimbach formed a white students union at Towson University, Maryland in 2012. The Southern Poverty Law Centre designated it a hate group.

Our new-found blindness to race doesn't blind us to racism. Racism remains, but not race. Having rejected race, we could just say racists are mistaken. We don't. While learning to pass people of other races without our European eyes confessing we've noticed them, we've lost the ability to let racist remarks pass without rebuke. If any of us don't reject all notions of race, then someone else brings us back into line. We haven't moved beyond racial identities enough to be indifferent to white people retaining them. Becoming disinterested in race, we've become transfixed with racism.

Being white is being unable to see ourselves as other races see themselves. No matter how few we become, we rationalise our rejection of only our racism by insisting that ours remains the dominant culture, but in increasing numbers of places it clearly doesn't. Not simply a minority as we are in Texas, we're no longer the largest minority in California or New Mexico. I'm not sure we've ever been the largest minority in Hawaii. We still don't allow ourselves racial loyalties or begrudge the more numerous Hispanics or Asians theirs. We respect other races' loyalties, unacceptable for us.

At Georgia State University by 2013, white people comprised only thirty-eight percent of students. "If we are already minorities on campus and are soon to be minorities in this country, why wouldn't we have the right to advocate for ourselves and have a club just like every other minority?" asked eighteen-year-old freshman Patrick Sharp, who tried to form a white students union. "All we want to do is celebrate white identity. This is about being in touch with who you are as a white person and being proud of that."

We're not proud. Among other races around us, we think we can hide.

2. WHITE MAN'S BURDEN

Focused upon betterment instead of equality, my forebears went out from Britain to benefit Britain but also to aid the rest of the world, however much we now find that hard to believe. *"I am only determined to go on and to do all I can while able for the poor degraded people of the north,"* Scottish missionary and explorer David Livingstone wrote from South Africa (referring to the rest of Africa, not Bradford), in a letter to the Reverend Richard Cecil on the eleventh day of July 1842. Livingstone famously became lost during his mission to help the Africans' lot, and the letter was among many relics of our long Western history displayed at the National Library of Australia a hundred and seventy years later.

In February 1899, towards the end of the centuries in which Europeans spread civilisation around the world, Englishman Rudyard Kipling wrote his poem 'The White Man's Burden' for Queen Victoria's Diamond Jubilee, although it was first published with the subtitle 'The United States and the Philippine Islands.' Sincerely or satirically, he exhorted Europeans nobly sacrificing so much to assist other races. *"Go make them with your living,"* he cried, *"And mark them with your dead."*

Unable to care for themselves, Kipling mused, they needed us. We helped them, dying as we did, even if they hated us for it. Our greatest fault was arrogance. It still is.

More than a century onwards, we no longer want our old-fashioned empires but, with our certain self-assurance, still carry the world's problems on our shoulders. Other races are no less aware than we are of wars, poverty, and pestilence elsewhere, but only we think our role is to solve them. I've done it myself.

Adopting other people's problems as our own, we work to earn money and send it away, providing for people we've never met. Bearers of our white man's burden, we dispense payments from our bank accounts or credit cards to relieve impoverished other races and aid victims of distant disasters we've seen on the television news. Our causes are in countries we can't find on maps.

We've done something more. Few images from my childhood were as frightening as those broadcast from one particular episode of the twenty-six episode British television series *The World at War*: grainy black-and-white images broadcast and rebroadcast tens of thousands of times since 1945. Excruciatingly thin men and women, their pallid flesh dangling from their skeletons, shuffled around the concentration camps of Europe. Stood naked, too weary to flee, they were shot dead, their bodies falling to their graves. Bulldozers shovelled up scores of corpses. Others were incinerated in ovens. Not being Jewish didn't diminish its significance. I had no reason to know those victims mightn't be me.

In response to National Socialism, Nazism, and the Second World War, the West embraced international socialism, rejecting the nationalism while adopting the socialism. We ceased striving to improve our people's lot in life but became obsessed with equality and pursuit of still more, especially racial equality. Ours isn't the socialism of common purpose and ownership within a race, as it was in Nazi Germany and remains among other rich races and the nationalist communism in Asia. Our interracial socialism is the socialism of sameness.

We never ceased being conscious of race. We became selective about when we think of it. Through all the lenses by which we look upon people, we're much further than we admit from blinding ourselves to race. Unable to end racial thinking, our best efforts can't strip the reality of racial difference from our eyes. Race remains inescapable: the crux of our dilemma.

Knowing we can't ignore race, we remain other races' benefactors. The races we refuse to countenance benefiting us, we recognise to benefit them. While we lambaste white people proud of their race, we applaud those concerned other races are still poorer, sicker, or stupider than we are. Our postmodern social conscience is one for other races more than our own: a burden collective upon the West and individual upon each of us. We consider caring about our races to be racist, but helping other races to be humanitarian. Basking in our white people's burden, we're not sure what we'd do without it.

William Easterly's 2006 book *The White Man's Burden: Why the West's Efforts to Aid the Rest Have Done So Much Ill and So Little Good* reported Western governments had spent more than two trillion

American dollars on foreign aid through the preceding five decades, although I've never heard anyone applaud that we give so much. No race in history has sought to do more good for more people than have Europeans. He blamed our failure to achieve very much on our failure to respect and empathise with the recipients, but paternalism underpins our white people's burden. The failure was our fault.

Only we talk in terms of rich countries being obliged to help poor countries. We set minimum targets, most commonly half of one percent of gross domestic product, presuming that only we are so rich, along sometimes with Japan, although I've never heard anyone remark upon the level of Japanese aid. Only we feel moral obligations to other races.

The people we help don't enter into it. We keep being generous because it's our post-racial identity, as much as it was once a feature of our racial identity. Among the many colourful cloth badges my wife sewed onto our daughters' girl guides blankets are ones picturing stylised hands marked *"Our rights"* and *"Our responsibilities."* The hand adjoining the rights is dark. The hand adjoining the responsibilities is pale. Rights are for other races. We have obligations. By thinking we're obliged to help other races, within our countries and without, we don't sense our goodness.

Other races aren't interested in equality, unless it betters them. They don't want the equality that would bring their people down.

Their countries aid foreigners not from any sense of obligation or equality but to further their national objectives and interests. The China Young Volunteers Association sends young Chinese to do development work in countries with governments friendly to China, like Laos, Ethiopia, and Burma.

The Japanese built a lovely airport at Apia, with terminals in the style of old Samoan villages, conducive to Japanese businessmen and tourists. It was also nice for me visiting there in 1987, when I imagined the Samoans most likely to use it were those emigrating. We feel ashamed when the foreign aid we give conveys any incidental benefit to us, but contracting our companies to help other races lets us spend more.

Tiny Luxembourg is the richest country on earth per capita, but burgeoning economic growth has made populous China and India richer overall. The only oil in Luxembourg is the petrol in very clean stations and very nice cars, but oil has made other countries rich. The second and third richest countries per capita are Equatorial Guinea and the United Arab Emirates. While the West gives our money away, rich Arab emirates indulge themselves. Along with an indoor ski resort and underwater hotel, one building in Dubai overtook another as the tallest building on earth.

Oil-rich Arab countries can be generous donors, but only to fellow Arabs and Muslims. Saudi Arabia spent more than eighty-seven billion American dollars from 1973 to '97 to build and maintain over fifteen hundred mosques, two hundred and two colleges, two hundred and ten Islamic centres, and almost two thousand schools educating Muslim children in Europe, the Americas, Australasia, and Asia.

European peoples would have welcomed such loyalty from us. In 2006, America donated almost twenty-three billion dollars to foreign countries, with Jewish Israel and Arab Egypt the main recipients. She gave a hundred and sixty-three million dollars to little black Haiti and a hundred and forty-five million dollars to black Ethiopia, but only fifty-two million dollars supporting democracy in sprawling Russia and a hundred and fifteen million dollars to massive Ukraine.

Arabs discriminate, but they're planning for their future after oil. We're not planning for a future at all. Amidst our spiralling national debts and financial crises since 2008, the West rarely questions whether we should keep giving money away. In 2011, while cutting pensions for her people, Britain increased foreign aid for others.

We're unashamedly racial with our generosity, providing aid with full regard to the races of the recipients, but they're not our races. When the United Nations wanted the West to do more to help Africans the world over, it declared 2011 to be International Year of African Descendants, although a year didn't satisfy the Africans. The First World Summit of African Descendants, in August that year, wanted ten years. It concluded with a 'Declaration of the Decade of African Descendants and the creation of a new fund for Afro-descendant Development.'

Our helping hands we offer other races. Offering them to our own would be racist.

Describing the collapse of Mozambique through the past twenty years, American economist Douglas Casey wrote in 1996 of the poor country elite *"who were able to systematically loot their countries* *and salt away the proceeds in Switzerland. That's where all the foreign aid (which might be defined as a transfer from poor people in rich countries to rich people in poor countries) went as well. The U.S. government still squanders about $20 billion a year this way, and European governments spend proportionally even more; it's all gone straight down a giant rat hole."* (Casey didn't say it, but Mozambicans might've fared better under Portuguese colonialism than independence we funded.)

Most significant was Casey's aside. The costs of our racial generosity and grand social consciences aren't borne by our rich but our poor, who forgo opportunities for better healthcare, education, and housing so we can give them to others. We don't identify with the rest of our race, so don't feel like we're giving our wealth away. Our rich and middle classes might suffer a little more taxes, but we're redistributing wealth we don't notice; we mightn't be rich but don't feel like we're poor. We can afford generosity with other people's money: socialism for a socialist aristocracy. The white people's wealth we're most keen to redistribute is the wealth of other white people.

The beneficiaries of our foreign aid aren't primarily the poor of other races but the elite. No wonder rich people from rich and poor countries alike want us to give more.

We share our national good with other races, embracing them when we're liking our countries, but keep our obligations to ourselves. Our racial identity is grounded not just in obligation but shame whenever we fall short. When our images of other race heroes and heroines give way to thoughts of their health, alcoholism, imprisonment, child abuse, and school truancy, then only we are responsible. We ask nothing of the indigenous drug addicts, alcoholics, and bums staggering around Alice Springs whenever I've been there. They remain absolved of obligation, enjoying only our sympathies.

The common caption in 2013 Australia was to *"Close the Gap,"* which I first saw on a large sticker affixed to the rear bumper of a car driving through wealthy Turramurra. It later adorned tee shirts of people haranguing passers-by through Martin Place, the second Thursday in June. The gap wasn't the huge amounts of extra time, money, and effort we already expended on indigenous people's health, but their poor health nevertheless. In spite of our great efforts, we feel we should do more; our sense of being white brings us no end of angst. We can't do enough.

We've become the people who hate us because the darker people's skin, the greater the mess of their lives. We have racial shame in abundance but can't imagine racial loyalty. We take responsibility for the failings of our democratically elected governments even if those governments reflect our multiracial citizenry or act outside the mandate of any election. When we're to blame for our inevitable failings, then we blame each other.

We held America's President George W. Bush responsible for Hurricane Katrina's devastating impact in 2005, accusing him of caring less about New Orleans than other American cities because it was principally black. We didn't blame the black city mayor, the looters, the one third of the city police force who failed to appear at work and some of whom became looters, or the residents who failed to heed the hurricane warnings beforehand.

Now I really enjoyed my three days in New Orleans, six years before the hurricane came, with a vibe that reached from the darkest and dustiest jazz rooms through the streets of a still Sunday morning. Gentrified black men with their grandfatherly hats made wonderful music seem effortlessly easy, although years of passion and practice preceded my time there. No one said a white man, let alone a white president, was responsible for that.

Not only are we kind to everyone else, we're horrible to each other. We're more arrogant than ever to see ourselves rising above race.

People are rational, up to a point, and our presumption they can't rescue themselves tells them they can't. If they don't need to strive then they won't. We don't.

American assistant secretary of labour Daniel Patrick Moynihan wrote in 1964 that "*the greatest single danger facing the Negroes of America is that the whites are going to put them on welfare…. We will have created an entire subculture of dependency, alienation, and despair….As against giving men proper jobs and a respectable place in their community and family*."

Australian Aborigines were renowned as good stockmen, for which they earned money and received food and board like other station-hands. When the Australian government began giving Aborigines what they called sit-down money without them needing to work, it culturally ravaged their communities.

If we tell people they're not accountable for their actions, they're not, but we hold only other races incapable of helping themselves. The beneficiaries of our burden might already be rich, but all the more credit to them for working hard and being clever, overcoming their affliction. They haven't chosen their race any more than we chose ours. It's the most perverse white supremacy, while we loathe our past racism.

In practice, white supremacy has become another label to abuse white people not hating their race. So sure have we become that all races are equal, our races can't have prospered so well in the past because of our ingenuity, enterprise, or hard work. We can't have succeeded by our science, engineering, or innovation. No mental or physical superiority could've let us conquer the earth with grand empires. The only explanation remaining is our past oppression of others. Oppression by race, we call racism.

We discard our forebears' good characters in a grand generalisation they were bad, as we would never accept about other races. We damn ourselves for success.

When we blame our racism for other races' failings and misadventures, we increase our burden to compensate. When other races blame our racism, they lighten their burden, reducing their responsibilities. Florida congresswoman Frederica Wilson listed racism among the causes of a forty percent unemployment rate among black Americans less than thirty years of age, in a television interview the penultimate Monday of August 2011. Black unemployment was white America's fault.

Driving our foreign, economic, and social policy, it's only fair we thieves give away our ill-gotten inheritances, be it through welfare, immigration, or commerce. Other races aren't beneficiaries of our benevolence but victims. Payments to them aren't presents but reparations.

White people willing to work and subsidise other races by taxation and donation can't make equal what is unequal; centuries spent helping other races haven't made much improvement with some. Racial equality is an insatiable desire we can never discharge; our white man's burden never ends.

What we feel about races we should feel about individuals, if we insist everyone's equal. If our race can't have succeeded so well by our innate abilities or diligence but by exploiting others, then neither can one person succeed except by exploiting another. Karl Marx understood as much when he developed communism (totalitarian socialism) in the nineteenth century, interpreting differences by class much as we now think about differences by race. Embracing international socialism makes little sense without embracing socialism locally. Racial equality requires it.

We confuse justice with equality. Espousing equality creates feelings of injustice among people less intelligent, talented, or hard-working than others, while imposing the injustice of taking from the smarter, more skilled and more industrious to give to the rest. With our silver lapel pins and brooches, rich white individuals mightn't keep being so benevolent when the last wealth to give up is ours.

3. OTHER RACES

In 2011 and '14, two different Australian governments proposed referenda recognising Aborigines and Torres Strait Islanders in the Australian Constitution: a recognition and reverence afforded no other race. In another of our racial paradoxes, the 2011 government also proposed a referendum to remove section 51 (xxvi) from the Constitution, which had been innocuous in 1901. *"The Parliament shall, subject to this Constitution, have power to make laws for the peace, order, and good government of the Commonwealth with respect to… (xxvi) The people of any race, for whom it is deemed necessary to make special laws."*

Of all the races in which colonial Europeans throughout the countries we colonised take refuge since rejecting our race, no choices are more popular than our indigenous peoples. The Imparja Cup competition played each February in Alice Springs is reserved to indigenous cricketers. We're rather affectionate for their well-defined races.

Our contradictions around race continue. Indigenous people can be described by their race, without talk of nationality, birthplace, or citizenship. Aborigines aren't just Australians or Aboriginal Australians but Aborigines or Koori, unless there's a specific point to be made. Torres Strait Islanders aren't Torres Strait Islander Australians, unless we think the extra word affirms their case to get something other Australians get, or be something other Australians are.

Native New Zealanders are Maoris. Other Western countries haven't gone fully the way of Americans with their Native Americans, but Aborigines aren't far shy of them. Native Australians sounds too primitive. We're not even sure about calling Aborigines tribes, as Native Americans do. It might be construed as disrespectful.

Conversely, the rest of us aren't really Australians, New Zealanders, Americans, or Canadians. Indigenous peoples agree.

Many a form my wife and I complete for our children's

preschool, schooling, and other activities includes a section asking if we're Aborigines or Torres Strait Islanders; being indigenous are the last races individuals can be. The questions aren't any Naziesque effort to ostracise anyone but if they're not gathering data about race and often even if they are, an invitation to participate in government or other assistance. No wonder our children, for the sake of getting that assistance, sometimes said they wished we were Aboriginal.

"Can you tell?" asked a large colourful poster in the staff area of the Hornsby and Ku-ring-gai Hospital, the first Sunday in July 2013. *"Aboriginal and Torres Strait Islander people come in different shapes, sizes & shades. Ensure you ask every patient…. Aboriginality: don't forget to ask."* Issuing the poster weren't just the Aboriginal Medical Service but also the Northern Sydney, South Eastern Sydney, and Sydney Local Health Districts.

The Participant Details Form for the National Bowel Screening Programme in 2012 asked whether participants were Aboriginal or Torres Strait Islander, and also whether we were South Sea Islanders. If there was no racial link in the bowel cancer tests, then there might have been in the treatments.

Unlike our recognition of indigenous peoples, we normally recognise immigrants only in abstract, without noticing individuals. When first I visited America, on a business trip in September 1995, I remarked to the manager of the company's New York ferry business that I was surprised to see so many Asians. "I hadn't noticed," replied Mark. A Harvard Business School graduate, he really hadn't.

We are blind to race in even the most insignificant of contexts. Gathering at the Greengate Hotel, Killara after my friend Ashley's mother's funeral in December 2020, Ashley's wife Heather asked me what I thought of the priest's homily at the funeral. I answered that I struggled to understand him.

"What was that accent?" asked Heather. "Was it East European?"

The person beside her pointed out that the minister was Chinese. Thus the accent was Chinese.

Father Ernest Chau was not part Chinese. He was wholly Chinese. In spite of sitting in the pews before him for more than an hour, never more than five yards or so from him, and possibly seeing him before or after the service too, Heather had not noticed his race.

Like Mark, Heather was intelligent with good sight and hearing. She too was white.

Censuses around the world assist governments planning social services and other matters of state by asking people their age, gender, work and so forth, but no Australian census asked about race until 2001. Australian governments had little idea of the proportions of races among the populace, but some Australians complained asking people their ancestry in the 2001 census was divisive. No school forms ask whether we're Asian, African, or Middle Eastern as they ask whether we're Aboriginal or Torres Strait Islander.

Our refusal to recognise individual racial identities doesn't deter other races from doing so. Born in New York, Puerto Rican wasn't simply Sonia Sotomayor's heritage. It was her identity. If not Puerto Rican, she was Newyorkrican, or Nuyorican.

Sotomayor was proud of what race could mean. 'A Latina Judge's Voice,' she titled her 2001 annual Judge Mario G. Olmos Law and Cultural Diversity Lecture at Berkeley Law School, University of California, saying "our gender and national origins may and will make a difference in our judging... I would hope that a wise Latina woman with the richness of her experiences would more often than not reach a better conclusion than a white male who hasn't lived that life... Personal experiences affect the facts that judges choose to see."

We normally mention immigrant races only in the context of something good to say. Reports of Sonia Sotomayor's nomination to become a judge on the American Supreme Court in 2009 never failed to mention she was Hispanic or Latina.

With identity comes money. In 2014, the Australia-Vietnam Education Promotion Association began offering university scholarships reserved to students of Vietnamese origin. Birthplace was immaterial; students could be Australian born or not. Citizenship was immaterial; students could be Australian citizens or not. Language and other culture were immaterial; students might have been unable to speak or read Vietnamese and known nothing of Vietnamese culture. Being racially Vietnamese was the eligibility criterion.

There is a world of race and races indifferent to what white people think of identity. While we dedicate government departments to immigrants, the Indian government dedicates a ministry to émigrés and their descendants who have never so much as visited India. By 2010, there were fifty million non-resident Indian citizens. Indians enjoy their racial identity beyond mere nationality as the West understands. However many races make up India, theirs is a racial loyalty to those who've not seen India for generations. It's not a cultural loyalty dependent upon whether people like curry.

I became aware of the Global Organisation of People of Indian Origin in 2009 when residents of Punjab Place in Logan, Queensland signed a petition to change its name to Oak Tree Place. "This isn't racist," insisted resident Ron Edmonds. "Oak Tree is just a nicer name."

"I'm a proud Punjabi," defiantly responded property developer Manjit Bopirai, who'd named the street four years earlier. "It's just a name we like, and it lets everyone know we are successful people." Living in the West hadn't affected his racial identity. "It's our heritage, it's our money. We can name it whatever we like." He wasn't Australian. "I have never called Australia a racist country but in this instance I will. These elderly people just want to make a noise."

Deriding elderly Australians didn't bother Bopirai, but our submission to accusations of racism meant the residents withdrew their petition. Punjab was an "Indian name," said resident Annie Liu, as white people wouldn't dare; she needn't fear accusations of racism. "It is not against Indians, but this is a beautiful street and Oak Tree is a beautiful name."

Few countries outside the West spruik diversity, and they're the diversities of people who've been there for centuries. India's racial diversity is much less than its differences with peoples outside South Asia.

Other countries becoming independent after World War II were already a potpourri of different races. Indonesia adopted the slogan "Unity in Diversity" trying to hold together the most artificial of multinational superstates reaching across islands and portions of them. Subsequent invasion and annexation added to the diversity of distinctive homelands of peoples, with racial and religious lines dividing along geography, except where the dominant Javanese moved in.

I once heard talk of the paler brown-skinned Javanese looking down upon darker brown-skinned Timorese (and presumably Melanesians in Irian Jaya). Accompanying it was a remark that all races look down upon races darker than they are.

Unimaginable as it would be in the West, Singaporean national identification cards specify a person's race or mix of races. "In multiracial Singapore," explained Ho Peng Kee, senior minister of state for home affairs in 2010, "we still need the race classification. We celebrate our diversity and this is our strength. So unlike other societies, for example in France, to be politically correct, they do away with recording and reflecting race...but that does not mean that the problems will go away."

Singapore may well celebrate diversity, because it's too small an island for there to have been a Singaporean race. Without the British Empire allowing an infusion of other races, Singapore would've been part of neighbouring Malaysia much longer than just the two years to 1965. There are Singaporean Chinese, Singaporean Malays, and so forth, but no Singaporean Singaporeans.

Nor are there Malaysian Malays, just Malays. Multiracial Malaysia speaks of Malaysian Chinese and Malaysian Indians: citizens born in Malaysia, as their parents and grandparents were. They aren't Chinese Malaysians or Indian Malaysians, as we would refer to them in the West.

Race is their identifying noun. Their birthplace, citizenship, and residency are merely descriptive adjectives, when the racial noun is inadequate. My friend Ted's wife was Malaysian Chinese before becoming Australian Chinese. All races on earth do the same when speaking to both race and residency, except us.

We used to. The last Saturday before Christmas 2008, standing in the Learn 4 Fun toyshop at the Macquarie Centre, I overheard a youthful customer inquire of two young saleswomen whether they thought the person for whom he contemplated buying a particular game or toy would understand its Australian nuances. "She's an A.B.C.," he explained, using a term I'd not heard for years. "Do you know what that means?"

A saleswoman replied with a confidence to mean he should have known she knew. "Australian-born Chinese," she answered. All three were white.

I'm sure the old A.B.C. milk bar in Hornsby was so named because the man operating it was an A.B.C., whose forebears could have come to Australia as long ago as the nineteenth-century gold rushes. An Australian-born Briton would've been a tautology, much like a New Zealand-born Briton, American-born European, or Canadian-born Briton, Frenchman, or Frenchwoman. An Australian-born German wasn't an A.B.G. but Australian and German.

National borders can seem artificial, particularly when they're not being enforced. They don't make people into something they're not.

When we in the West relegated race to the background, the defining noun became a descriptive adjective (if we mention race at all). Race (or whatever moniker we use to mean race) became adjectival: a mere descriptor of a person, like being tall or short. Nationality became, to us, more important than race; the adjective became the noun. We might hyphenate the words, placing the nationality noun last. If people are anything more particular than all the people on earth, then citizenship defines them.

People became Chinese Australians, African Americans, and so forth, whether newly inducted citizens or locally born. If they move elsewhere, they become another clumsy hybrid. Africans in the Caribbean are Afro-Caribbean, so when they immigrate to Britain they're Afro-Caribbean British. If that's too much to say, they're Afro-Caribbean, but still British.

We're the people without adjectives beyond being white, although we don't think much about it. Being white is not being anything else.

In 1998, Sacha Molitorisz wrote of tribalism being rife among young people in Sydney. Being blind to race, he described fourteen tribes typically defined by people's jobs, although some people straddled several tribes. Chris Wirasinha called himself a Slashie, "As in, I'm a D.J.-slash-filmmaker-slash-photographer."

Over the ensuing ten years, several tribes dissipated. Others arose. The list I read in 2010 was of eight tribes, none of which jobs defined. Race didn't name any, but quietly defined at least some. "There are Arab groups where it would be hard for a non-Arab to join," let slip seventeen-year-old Adam Osman, an Egyptian in the Gangstas with Lebanese and New Zealander friends, "but not impossible."

Seventeen-year-old Abdul Skaf loved the beach, camping, and the Canterbury Bulldogs rugby league team, wanting to be a police officer. He was born in Australia and didn't want to live anywhere else, but still found it hard to call himself Australian. "If someone asks me my nationality, I'm Lebanese," he said, "but when my parents tell me to be proud to be Lebanese, I tell them I'm Australian."

"When other people ask my nationality," said Australian-born Laryn Zabakly, seventeen years old, "I tell them the full thing, Syrian–Jordanian–Armenian, but when my parents tell me I'm Arabic, I tell them 'Nup, I'm Australian'." She went onto explain, "You can't give up your background, where your parents come from. Being Australian is not all of who you are. Why can't you just be all of it?"

To Zabakly, an Australian was a "blond surfie boy with the Southern Cross tattooed on him." She made me seem not Australian.

Fourteen-year-old Cansu Sevinc left Turkey when she was five. "Turkish," she said of herself. "I'm proud to be a Turk."

In 2010, a study of three hundred and thirty-nine young people aged fourteen to seventeen years old in the western and south-western suburbs of Sydney found that only a third of them identified as being Australian, in spite of two thirds of them being born here and the majority feeling good about living here. They particularly liked Australia's friendliness, respect for others, and freedom of choice, but still identified themselves by what journalist Adele Horin called their ethnic background: Tongan, Chinese, Lebanese, and so forth. Less than half of them also felt Australian all the time and one-fifth did not feel Australian at all.

They had friends from many races, but none had close friends from what Horin called Anglo backgrounds. Sevinc said she might feel more Australian if people from "outside suburbs were more open and friendly."

They felt at home in their ethnic neighbourhoods and sometimes felt uneasy elsewhere. "I'm more comfortable here than in, say, North Sydney," said Zabakly, sitting with two other teenagers in the Home Bass Youth Cafe in Bankstown.

Economist Jock Collins at the University of Technology, Sydney, didn't see any problem in those young people's unwillingness to identify as Australian. "A lot of these young people…have diverse and multiple identities," he said. "They incorporate their migrant identities with elements of being Australian."

He was being polite. Collins saw the challenge as being to promote a more diverse idea of what being Australian meant, which really meant being Australian means little at all.

Collins and the immigrants alluded to a common theme. Residency and nationality are merely points of distinction within races, distinguishing without dividing them. Our parents' and prior generations were the same. Outside their races, geography doesn't matter. Race defines them.

4. COMMUNITIES

During my time working at TNT Shipping & Development Limited, the monorail manager kept Scotch whisky in his offices for meetings with Lionel, a Chinese entrepreneur. Lionel responded to an offer of Johnnie Walker Red Label by saying he only used it for cooking, but nevertheless drank it. I hope at least one of the stories he told, of his involvement in deals worth hundreds of millions of dollars, was true.

Lionel's lawyers were Chinese. Through him and them, I met many more Chinese. I joined a group of them from a Chinese newspaper in a Chinese restaurant in Strathfield, where the only aspect of the night that wasn't expressly Chinese was the singing. We sang karaoke. "I write the songs…"

They were fun to be with, while our business dealings were always fair if not generous to them. When our business dealings concluded, the invitations ceased. I fell away from the network.

Just because we don't prefer the company of our race hasn't kept other races from preferring the company of theirs. Multiracial communities are a Western dream. Instead, there's a plethora of little indigenous and immigrant communities of men and women, boys and girls: pockets of parallel, sweet racial eddies, spinning around in small spaces. They gather among their kind, while solitary white folk frequent their restaurants.

If community means anything, it includes a sense of collective identity, with loyalties and sympathies. The quest for identity is the quest for community. The only people without communities are white. We're individuals. The individualism we require of ourselves, we don't require from other races.

White people avoid mentioning race when mentioning it would be racist. Other races aren't races but peoples. They're Somali, Samoan, and other communities, despite being so far from Somalia, Samoa, and so forth. We bandy about talk of community to describe other races as we would never talk of Europeans comprising communities, except in Europe. That's Europe defined not by race or a collection of races but by place of residence.

Below the road bridge outside the entrance to Redfern railway station is no river or park. There are train lines. Among the messages about drugs and condoms painted on the brick walls along the bridge, the last day of April 2009, was a plea for unity among Aborigines: an image contrasted "*Unity vs. Loneliness.*"

It could also be made among white people. If we can't find unity, we're lonely. We lose ourselves in alienation.

Other races have never been more emboldened. Standing on an escalator after leaving the Kinokuniya bookshop in Sydney, the evening of the third Tuesday of June 2011, I stood behind a young Chinese man and his Chinese girlfriend. On the back of his black tee shirt, in huge bright block lettering, were the words "*UNITY IS POWER.*"

Around us, as in so much of the city, the vast majority of people were Chinese. If they weren't Chinese, they were something else East Asian. This wasn't diversity. This was Asian.

Their unity was palpable. So was my individualism. I was powerless, as I wouldn't mind feeling in Asia, but I wasn't. I was in the city and land of my birth.

The essence of those two captions is the same. White people have no unity; that would be racism. We're lonely, without power.

I never heard anyone suggest racially homogenous countries are venues for dwindling hearts and withering humanness, but multiracial reality is racial ghettoes. "We tend to form clusters based on similarities," said Turkish writer Elif Shafak of multiracial Australia in 2010, "then we produce stereotypes about other clusters of people." If we remain within our tight circles, then our "hearts will dwindle and our humanness may wither."

We're supposed to think other races like diversity as much as we do. They don't.

During the year my youngest son attended preschool, two days a week, parents shared only one social function. In spite of so many children and parents being Asian, a mother organising the social function remarked that very few Asians came. She was being polite. None came, that I saw. "They didn't even bother replying" to the invitation, she said.

Being good white people, she and others in the conversation presumed few of those parents spoke English, but they must have seen those parents at preschool more often than I'd seen them.

They spoke English.

We've opened our lives to other races, as no others have. Few of them come. That's their right.

Through all the years of Christmas drinks at the preschool, the only parents I recall attending were white. A handful of other faces attended our children's primary and high school cocktail parties and trivia nights, but most were married to white people. Meredith insisted a black woman come with her to primary school events. They were far, far fewer than in the school playgrounds. Australian parents at my eldest two daughters' high school convened an Oriental Night trying to get Asian parents along. They still didn't come.

In my second daughter's first year of high school, the only parent who wasn't Western among the forty or so parents attending the Parents Summer Social evening was married to a white person. Instead of imagining that racial integration is our Western vision, white South African Catherine, who hosted the event with her husband, said she'd heard Asians like direct invitations instead of electronic mail sent to all parents.

"The company I work for is one third owned by the Chinese," I told her. "The Chinese go to Chinese community events organised by email."

Asians mightn't have attended school social events, but they were out in force for the Parent Information Evening for my eldest son's Higher School Certificate courses, part way through year ten, and other events focused upon their children's education, organised through electronic mail. They weren't fulfilling our fantasy of a multiracial community, but that didn't matter. We thought they were.

By my eldest son's last year of school, when each year had a parents' co-ordinator, Chinese parents had their own co-ordinator. A year later, Chinese and Korean parents each had their own parent information nights. If they gathered together socially, we never knew.

Immigrant children are like their parents, in spite of our presumption they'd become like us. My eldest daughter's friend Pansy was a rare Asian attending their year-eleven social event: a harbour cruise.

In 2011, while preparing for leadership training for our local cubs pack, I read of ethnic-based scouting: scout troops and packs dedicated to particular races (but not ours) and to Muslims. When white people gather by race, we call it racism. When other races gather by race, we call it ethnic based.

Indians in Australia formed the Resourceful Australian Indian Network in 2006, buying a house in Penshurst where about fifty elderly Indians gathered weekly. Not only do we respect such racial loyalties, we fund them. The New South Wales government gave the Indians more than fifteen thousand dollars under the Community Building Partnership programme in 2013.

It makes us all the more peculiar that we don't congregate by race. Theirs is the right of free association, to be among their race and to feel better about it. Whether it's merely a matter of taste, as human nature can be, or more, we only damn white people feeling the same, who would if they could.

Black American actor Laurence Fishburne claimed he could feel racism in the air when visiting Australia in 2000. Nothing was said, but he could feel what he called the "vibe." Then, "after the Olympics," he said, "a lot of people of colour arrived in Sydney…" He "decided 'This is nice, I'm going to stay here.' So instead of seeing the same five black faces in Sydney every day, I'd see two new black faces a week and that was nice."

Lesley Townsend was Aboriginal. She liked to live in what journalist Debra Jopson called Sydney's black urban heart: Redfern. "Whenever you work with another Koori," said Townsend, "you feel more contented, rather than being the odd one out. It is better to see another black face than a sea of non-Aborigines."

By 2010, the most common family names in Parramatta, the geographical heart of Sydney, were Patel, Singh, and Chen, according to the White Pages telephone directory. (Smith and Jones were no longer among the top twenty.) The *Daily Telegraph* newspaper merrily demonstrated the point with a photograph of Nikhil, Varad, Manish, Keshavlal, Sejal, Hemal, and Chintan Patel outside Patel Brothers supermarket, Harris Park. "It doesn't surprise me that Patel is the most popular last name in this area," said Manish, "you just have to look at what's happened in the US. They call motels over there 'Potels' because so many Patels are over there and running them."

In Cabramatta, it's the Nguyens, Trans, and Huynhs. At Lakemba, Kahn and Islam are among the most common. Cambodian, Senegalese, and scores more immigrant communities are just that, without meaningful relationships between them.

There's no racial integration but a natural segregation we aren't so racist as to notice, unless we like it. "It highlights what an amazing place metropolitan Sydney is today," enthused White Pages group manageress Jane Blackley. She forecast continuing growth in Asian names because of immigration, her British people abating.

At the end of the newspaper article, almost tinged with disappointment, came a qualification. *"But there remain some areas where the traditional Smiths, Joneses and Browns still dominate, such as Cronulla, Windsor and Campbelltown."*

In 2011, Wollondilly Shire Council had the lowest proportion of foreign-born residents of any Sydney local government area. Deputy mayor Benn Banasik didn't think that Sydney having become a city of enclaves was a problem. "...the key to successful integration, I believe, is not forcing new monocultures into areas which have a low proportion of Australians born overseas, but rather providing incentive for new Australians to bring aspects of their own culture to our outlying communities."

While we speak disparagingly of white streets, suburbs, and cities and the racism they imply, we rarely speak of them being of another race. We call them multicultural, which blinds us to how racially homogenous they are. *"People are naturally drawn to living among people similar to them,"* wrote Afghan lawyer Mariam Veiszadeh in 2011, *"whether because of ethnicity, class, or religious background."* They're never alone.

Money and other incentives lead people to emigrate to where they're racial minorities. There, they cluster by race. There's no melting pot; people don't want it. It's not white people's fault. It's not anybody's fault.

Campaigning for the 2012 elections, Washington councilman and former mayor Marion Barry recognised a lack of engagement between Asian businesspeople and Africans in his Southeast Washington ward. "We got to do something about these Asians coming in and opening up businesses and dirty shops," he complained. "They ought to go. I'm going to say that right now, but we need African American businesspeople to be able to take their places, too."

As well as his fellow councilmen condemning him was the abundance of racially based business organisations. Susan Au Allen, president of the Pan Asian American Chamber of Commerce, called Barry's comments "regrettably inappropriate. I'm hoping he misspoke."

"He's got one insensitive focus," said Minority Business Roundtable president Roger Campos, "and that's on African Americans solely and no other groups." He called Barry's remarks "totally insensitive. It's kind of interesting because Asians and Hispanics are fuelling the economy in business growth, and we ought to be inclusive of all minority groups, not just one."

Europeans had long become a minority in Washington. We still weren't a minority group.

Our embracing of other races doesn't mean they do. They'll assert their homogeneity, as we refuse to defend ours.

The Domain in Sydney is a large grassed area where Australians gather for everything from concerts to strangers standing on soapboxes to argue political opinions, but not the middle weekend of October 2013. *"Singapore Day aims to bring a slice of home to Singaporeans abroad so as to emotionally connect them back to Singapore,"* explained the website for the Overseas Singaporean Unit, which hired the venue. *"It is also an event to galvanise the Singaporean community so that the sense of identity and belonging remain strong."*

More than six thousand Singaporeans and their families came for the free event. Nobody else was allowed. *"There were no PRCs, India Indians, Bangla or Pinoys to annoy us,"* wrote one happy Singaporean, Anthony Sim, on his website afterwards. I had to research to discover Pinoys were Filipinos.

Australians mightn't have been annoying, but any trying to enter the Domain that day were refused admission. Telephone callers to radio station 2GB host Ben Fordham complained that "white people" had been "turned away in droves."

Each race gathers in its suburbs, its places to belong, but us. In 2012, the *Sydney Morning Herald* newspaper enthused about suburban Strathfield progressing through multiculturalism to becoming Korean. 'Little Korea ready to rise from melting pot,' said the headline. Social economist Jock Collins and Joon Shin, from the Cosmopolitan Civil Societies Research Centre at the University of Technology, Sydney, published a report saying the time had come to create Little Korea in Sydney, where more than a hundred and fifty thousand Koreans were thought to live.

Young Park, owner of the Doo Ri Korean barbecue restaurant,

said Strathfield was already Little Korea. "Food is a common bond," said Korean-born councillor Keith Kwon. Forty-nine food businesses were there. "It doesn't matter if it's Korean, Indian, or Chinese, when you eat the food you feel part of that community, but food should not be the end of it either."

Separations across our cities become confrontations across our neighbourhoods, when people get close. The only experience we've had of the Korean family living across the street from us, beyond the sights of their backyard barbecues at which the only guests are other Koreans or the sounds of instrument practice from their open windows, was the afternoon after school the third Friday of September, 2011. My twelve-year-old second daughter told me the Koreans had seen her playing with her siblings from their window. "They gave us the rude finger," she told me.

It could've been worse. We knew the Korean boy's name was Sung Wong, because he studied at our children's primary school. At the end of winter the previous year, three baby Hooded Plover birds nested with their eggs at the school. Sung Wong smashed their eggs and kicked the birds to death.

5. JEWISH IDENTITY

Just one Jewish grandparent would have made my friend Gregor Jewish under the Nuremberg race laws. He had three.

Gregor and his Jewish wife have two Jewish daughters, but the Jewish definition of being born a Jew is narrower than the Nazi German definition. Traditional Jewish law insists Gregor isn't a Jew because his maternal grandmother wasn't. That doesn't make Gregor Western. It makes him incomplete.

Nevertheless, Gregor considers himself Jewish because his father was Jewish. In our increasingly postmodern West, whatever Gregor considers himself to be, we believe him to be. We're not acceding to anyone's laws.

American film-maker Paul Mazursky was responsible for such films as *Bob & Carol & Ted & Alice*, which saw adultery as a step towards everyone loving each other. "I've always felt very Jewish but very ambivalent about being Jewish," he said, expressing as well as anyone the dichotomy between a profound consciousness of being racially Jewish without any pride or, for that matter, shame. Ambivalence is better than pain. "I'm an atheist," he said, while understanding that religion is an aspect of culture. "Yet wherever I travel, I always find a synagogue." Post-Jewish Jewry is Jewry nevertheless.

Mazursky was talking about a pilgrimage home to the land of his grandparents, Ukraine. "In my personal opinion," said spectacle maker David Miretsky, whose pilgrimage to Uman inspired Mazurksy, "Paul is an older gentleman reaching his ripe age, and he wanted to find his roots."

Photographer Annie Leibovitz also recognised the difference between Judaism the religion and Jews as a race. "I'm not a practising Jew," she said in 1994, "but I feel very Jewish."

Like other immigrants (even after more than a millennium in Europe), being Jews is the noun. Their birthplaces and citizenry are, if anything, mere adjectives. Ukrainian Jews aren't Jewish Ukrainians. They're not European (except adjectivally) or white.

They're Jewish or Jews.

For our part, we speak of Jewish communities, and not just in Israel, without presuming anything of their religious beliefs. We can thus only be speaking of race, although we hate ascribing the notion of race to Jews more than any other peoples; it brings back bad memories. We might mention them being of the Jewish faith, without regard for whether they really have faith. They're a collective people; we rarely label an individual a Jew or Jewess, although we're quick to call someone a Holocaust survivor or relation of Holocaust victims.

Sonja Abrahamsson learned as much when it was her turn to feed comments into the Swedish Tourism Board's public relations campaign for a week in 2012. Among a series of indecipherable, nonsensical messages, she challenged anti-Semitism, but did so mentioning Jews. *"What's the fuzz with jews. You can't even see if a person is a jew, unless you see their penises, and even if you do, you can't be sure!?"* She went onto point out that Nazi Germany required Jews to wear the Star of David so people could see who was a Jew. *"I'm sorry if some of you find the question offensive. That's was not my purpose. I just don't get why some people hates jews so much."*

Relatively restrained through the furore was Lindy West, editor of the *Jezebel* website catering to women. *"Okay,"* she wrote. *"Sooooo, I mean, awkward. Problematic. Not great. But at worst, Sweden Sonja sounds like a clueless, well-meaning bumpkin, and at best she's a cheery, state-sanctioned troll."*

Jews are the race that dares not speak its name, but Jews used to mention it. Groucho Marx rejected suggestions the 1933 Marx Brothers film *Duck Soup* had a political agenda by saying, "We were just four Jews trying to get a laugh."

Neither my Uncle Paul nor honorary Uncle Ivor ever spoke of being Jewish, although Ivor lamented that a Jewish friend's son had become a Christian. "The same thing happened to God," I smiled (before I'd thought about whether God and Jesus were Jewish). Ivor looked indignantly at me.

A few days after my mother's funeral, Ivor said some of the wisest and most helpful words I've heard in my life. "You don't ever get over the death of your mother," he told me. "You don't ever adjust to it. You can't ever fill the space in your life that she left, but you learn to live around it."

As Ivor had wanted, his funeral was a secular affair. When they died, Jews (like Europeans) were traditionally buried, but Ivor had wanted to be cremated. (That was after his death, not beforehand.) The Nazis showed similar disregard for Jewish tradition by cremating corpses in the extermination camps. The observation Ivor so kindly gave me regarding my mother's death hasn't been taken up by his people regarding the Holocaust: the *Shoah*.

Jews suffered much more under Nazism than under Soviet communism. East Europeans suffered much more under communism. Eastern Europeans thus dwell less upon the Jewish Holocaust than other European peoples do, but Jews allow them no excuse. They were furious at efforts in the early part of the twenty-first century in Lithuania to equate the two totalitarianisms, insisting that Lithuanians agree with them that Nazism was infinitely worse. Ultimately, the only basis for their claim was that Nazism targeted Jews.

All Jews are responsible for one another, says the Talmudic phrase *"Kol Yisreal Arevim Zeh beZeh,"* cited on the World Jewish Congress website in 2012. Founded in 1936, the congress' priorities remained anti-Semitism, the Holocaust legacy, Israel, and Jewish rights in Arab lands.

"The Holocaust is a very central element of the Israeli identity," said Israeli historian Tom Segev in March 2012. "There is not a single day without a reference to the Holocaust in the media…and there is not a single Arab leader who has not at some point been compared to Hitler. It is a very old cliché." What's true of Israel is true of the Jews.

Among the motivations for Segev's comments was Prime Minister Benjamin Netanyahu addressing American Israeli lobby group Aipac in Washington that month, when he held up a letter from the World Jewish Congress in 1944 urging America to bomb the Auschwitz concentration camp. The request, Netanyahu reminded them, was refused.

The long, dark shadow of Holocaust matters more to the West in retrospect than it did at the time. The only instant I recall comedian Marty Feldman being serious was talking about the wartime blitz of London. With his distinctively protruding eyes, he huddled among others in underground railway stations while German aircraft dropped their bombs overhead. There, he said later, Londoners abused him for being a Jew. If Englishmen and women blamed Jews for Britain declaring war upon Germany, that wasn't a reason to cease anti-Semitism. It was more reason to be anti-Semitic.

While Winston Churchill's views on race and culture have been labelled anti-Semitic by today's exacting standards, Churchill was not anti-Semitic. German businessman Ernst Hanfstaengl, a friend of Adolf Hitler before Hitler came to power and long before Churchill became British prime minister, wrote in his memoirs that Churchill said to him: "Tell your boss from me that anti-Semitism may be a good starter, but it is a bad sticker."

At a small afternoon party at my Jewish friend Ian Biner's home, sometime around about 1998, was a large and jovial fellow who befriended a Hispanic woman through a computer website, went to Texas to meet her, and married her. I remarked to him of British anti-Semitism and, in particular, Churchill's reputed anti-Semitism. "The difference was," the guest replied, "that the British weren't *killing* Jews."

He was right. We were killing Germans, but not to save Jews.

Ian never wavered in his Jewish identity, moulded by the Holocaust. He decided his fellow business development manager at Holyman Limited was anti-Semitic for being Latvian. The Germans' longest standing ally in Eastern Europe, since long before World War II, were the Latvians.

Ian described his first wife as "a typical Eastern-Suburbs Jewish princess." I never met her.

His later girlfriend Lisa was a Christian convert to Judaism when she married her first husband, remaining a Jewess after their divorce. Her wedding to Ian (the second for each of them) adopted the Jewish ritual of breaking glass, but wasn't in a synagogue. It was in a business club. She described Ian as "the most un-Jewish Jew" she knew.

"He's not," I said sadly, because any race not enjoying its culture saddened me. When Ian and Lisa feared her chemotherapy would leave her infertile, they contemplated adopting a poor child, an orphan I imagine, from India. Ian would doubtlessly have cared for the child, providing a fine private school education like his. Their home would be safe, somewhere in Australia, but not obviously Jewish.

My Jewish friend Rob (whose daughter was friends at school with my youngest daughter) didn't like shopping in St Ives, because of the South African Jews there. His girlfriend was Christian, and

Rob had no interest in teaching their daughter his people's culture; in their home stood a Christmas tree. If she were to have any religious education, Rob wanted her to learn a little of all religions and make up her mind.

"They're the words of an atheist," I told Rob. She would make up her own mind anyway, but without her parents offering her conviction. (It's not the approach we take to teaching children about race.)

I'd known Rob for years and we'd spoken of many things, without him hitherto alluding to the Holocaust. He spoke of beliefs getting Jews killed.

"Beliefs had nothing to do with it," I told him. "Atheists died in the Holocaust. It was all about race."

"Don't talk to me of the Holocaust!" he snapped, with a pain and fury from his core I'd never before seen. We never spoke of it again.

Sometime in my late teens, my neighbour Bruce's family (I think it was) possessed a book titled something like *Hitler Jude*. Jews who supported and collaborated with the Nazi regime have also been called Hitler Jews, but these were something else. Jews in Germany had lived like Germans with little thought of being Jewish until the rise of National Socialism and the Nazis coming to power in 1933.

In previous centuries, Jews had often escaped discrimination by changing their religion, or at least pretending to do so. That no longer worked, but they found amidst Nazi persecution their Jewish heritage, culture, and faith. They were again the chosen people of the Torah, and were punished for it. They were the Hitler Jews, who learnt to pray in the ghettos.

When the Second World War embroiled Europe, persecution became the Holocaust. If ever Jews were going to pray, they were praying in the death camps. Watching their hapless people die, they may well have begged the God of Moses to grant them another exodus. In the screams of others or screams of their own in their gas-chamber hell, they must've felt abandoned.

No amount of killing could change their Jewish race, but it could crush their Jewish faith. Jews who survived the Holocaust, and most of them did, their children and grandchildren, continue to feel abandoned. They're racially Jews but atheists or agnostics, if not completely indifferent to the notion of god. For the God of

Moses to have abandoned their people to Nazism, then the God of Moses wasn't there. That god died, or never was.

Theirs is a post-Jewish atheism, agnosticism, or indifference shaped by the Holocaust. No longer trusting god to save them, they strive to save themselves. Being Jewish is to do everything they can to keep Christian Europe and European peoples from harming them again.

A hunter should never wound a lion, or it will come back and kill him. Kill it or leave it be.

They're no longer *Hitler Jude*, but the legacy remains. European Jews have identity apart from being European. German Jews aren't German as much as Jews. Our Western post-racial vision is for Europeans, in Europe and elsewhere. Jews don't share that vision for themselves.

It's all a bit incongruous for the race at the forefront of ending European peoples' racial identities to retain racial identity for itself, but Jewish racism wasn't their problem. Our racism was. If there were really no race, if race were really an obsolete concept, then there'd be no Jewish race.

Being a Jew as a matter of race remains different to being a Jew as a matter of religion. American entertainer Sammy Davis, Junior described himself as "a one-eyed Jewish Negro" because he'd converted to the Jewish faith. It didn't deter him, in 1973, from accepting an invitation to join Anton LaVey's Church of Satan. LaVey (born Howard Levey) was a Jew.

When Shirli Kirschner, a Jewish lawyer turned mediator, told an audience at the new Sydney University Law School Open Day that she believed in social justice, she demonstrated the point by saying she helped indigenous people. Social justice didn't seem to mean helping poor Jews; she might've thought there weren't any.

Europeans aren't the only race keen to help other peoples; Jews are too. We're the only race feeling obliged.

With little policy beyond condemning President George W. Bush's war in Iraq and little experience of government, a young, black Illinois state senator delivered the keynote speech to the Democratic Party convention in 2004. Barack Obama spoke of his family history and implored America to find unity in diversity. Afterwards, film industry mogul David Geffen telephoned Obama. "You're going to run for president," he told him, "and I'm going to support you."

The two groups after African Americans giving Obama the largest majorities electing him president in 2008, with more than seventy percent of their votes, were Jews and homosexuals. Geffen was both. They normally favoured Democrats anyway, although not so substantially. Neither identify with white America.

Among all the Jews who, at least in some inadvertent recesses of their minds, acknowledged they were Jewish, I've known very few to be religiously devout. A rabbi friend of my father lamented the lack of anti-Semitism in Australia because he thought anti-Semitism would encourage Jews to find their faith, as it did in Nazi Germany. More damaging than persecution is tolerance.

6. JEWISH THEMES

Immediately after World War II, Jewish composer Richard Rodgers and half-Jewish lyricist Oscar Hammerstein wrote their 1949 song 'You've Got to Be Carefully Taught' and musical *South Pacific*. They reduced race to skin colour and eye shape, insisted people were born without racism, and accused Americans wanting to marry within their race of hating everyone else. "To hate all the people your relatives hate, you've got to be carefully taught."

Suddenly, racial discrimination was wrong. Eradicating white racism, ripping away our racial gestalt, would avert another Holocaust, at least one premised upon race.

George Seaton was Roman Catholic, but he grew up in a Jewish neighbourhood in Detroit and called himself a *"Shabbas goy,"* performing tasks for Jews they couldn't perform for religious reasons. He wrote and directed the 1950 film *The Big Lift*, which preached American democracy against German Nazism and Russian communism. It also preached racial integration. In a highly contrived, fictitious story set against historical fact (the Berlin Blockade of 1948 and '49), German woman Gerda told American airman Hank Kowalski that the Russians called Americans hypocrites. "You fought Hitler because he was against the Jews."

"Now, wait a minute," replied Hank. "That's only one of the reasons."

"Yes, but still you hated him for it, and the Russians say in America Jews are kept out of certain jobs, schools…"

"And they're right, it shouldn't be. It stinks."

Yet, the Hillcrest Country Club for the Hollywood film-making elite allowed only Jews to be members. Several members threatened to resign if it didn't admit Seaton.

Jewish screenwriter Walter Bernstein was responsible for the original script of the 1960 American film *The Magnificent Seven*. Quite apart from the theme music being among the most recognised scores while I was growing up (for being used in cigarette commercials), the film was probably the best known

Western. Before saving a Mexican village from Mexican bandits, heroes Chris Adams and Vin respond to white Americans discriminating against an Indian by shooting them.

The Indian was already dead. Brynner and McQueen's characters demanded racial integration in a cemetery.

Those wrongdoers didn't hate anyone. They simply differentiated their race from others.

American Jewish writer Samuel Fuller, whose parents were Russian Jews who'd changed their name from Rabinovitch, portrayed prostitution and child molestation beneath pretty American suburbia in his 1964 film *The Naked Kiss*. Central to a former prostitute's redemption was working, and singing, at a hospital treating handicapped children of all races and religions.

Austrian Jew Billy Wilder arrived in America in the 1930s and would go onto write and direct some of the best films I've seen, including my favourite film as I mature, *Sunset Boulevard*, in 1950. In his 1966 film *The Fortune Cookie*, investigator Chester Purkey knew he could goad cameraman Harry Hinkle into physical violence by making derogatory remarks about black Americans. It worked, allowing Hinkle to declare his moral core defending other races and withdrawing from the fraud that was central to the film.

In a film in which most central characters were to one degree or another greedy, although curiously likeable, easily the most honest and honourable was black American footballer "Boom Boom" Jackson. He suffered most from his friend Hinkle's fraud, for which Hinkle felt ashamed.

Another of my favourite writers for his work on the television series *The Twilight Zone*, with its well-crafted short stories around imaginative ideas and elegant twists, was American Jew Rod Serling. Being broadcast around the time I was born, I didn't see the series until two or three decades later. Like so many other memorable episodes, the fourth-season episode 'He's Alive' in 1963 was set in a present-time generalised America, in this case the suburbs. Serling introduced a young, blond American with the Germanic name Peter Vollmer: "a sparse, little man who feeds off his self-delusions and finds himself perpetually hungry for want of greatness in his diet, and like some goose-stepping predecessors, he searches for something to explain his hunger, and to rationalise why a world passes him by without saluting."

Inspired by a shadowy figure, Vollmer leads a small Nazi group.

After an elderly Jew denounces him, we the audience slowly see the shadowy figure behind him: a man we all thought died in 1945, Nazi German dictator Adolf Hitler.

"Where will he go next," asked Serling, in his closing narration to the episode, "this phantom from another time, this resurrected ghost of a previous nightmare? Anyplace, everyplace, where there's hate, where there's prejudice, where there's bigotry, he's alive."

Serling was telling us that not only could Germans commit a Holocaust. Americans and other European peoples could too, if we're not kind to other races. We believed him, all becoming perpetrators and potential recidivists.

"He's alive so long as these evils exist," continued Serling, describing white racial prejudice. "Remember that when he comes to your town. Remember it when you hear his voice speaking out through others. Remember it when you hear a name called, a minority attacked, any blind, unreasoning assault on a people or any human being. He's alive because through these things, we keep him alive."

I'm not the only person to have watched the 1980 American film *The Blues Brothers* many times over. The forces gathered against our heroes included the police, a country music band, a bar manager, a psychotic past girlfriend, and Nazis, led by a short blond twit and his homosexual sidekick. Jake Blues told his brother, "I hate Illinois Nazis."

John Landis, another American Jew, directed and was one of the writers of the film. The next film he directed was *An American Werewolf in London*, which had nothing to do with Nazis or Germans when I saw it in an Australian cinema. Twenty years later, I bought a disc-recording of it for my family and me to watch in our home, bouncing though the good humour, music, and frights, until there came a scene that Australian cinemas hadn't shown: a horrifying dream sequence in which a family watching television in its lounge room is suddenly massacred by Nazi monsters toting machine guns, blasting away the family menorah.

The scene scared the willies out of us, but had nothing to do with the rest of the film. Landis was born five years after World War II ended, but said Nazis and the Holocaust were part of his Jewish experience growing up. We haven't watched the film again.

Perhaps *When Harry Met Sally* in 1989 was the film about which I first heard someone refer to racial and religious prejudice being a

Jewish theme. Other commentators, such as Jewish writer Aire Kaplan, have made the same observation. The haunting experiences shared by disparate Jews and Jewesses left them determined their people not suffer another Holocaust.

In 1981, writer Lawrence Kasdan and director Steven Spielberg, both Jews, recreated 1930s film serials (the idea pitched to them by a Methodist, George Lucas) with *Raiders of the Lost Ark*. World War II hadn't yet broken out, but a thoroughly enjoyable hero was already fighting villainous Nazis.

The sequel, *Indiana Jones and the Temple of Doom*, offered South Asian villains, although far more South Asian heroes and victims. For the next sequel, *Indiana Jones and the Last Crusade*, Spielberg and Lucas rejected a script in which Jones fought a monkey prince in Africa because of its negative African stereotypes. Instead, Spielberg made another film about swarms of bad and bumbling Germans, in which a Christian brotherhood was willing to murder the hero. That was justified prejudice, warranted by the Jewish Holocaust as other prejudice wasn't (although we thought anti-Semitism was justified until the Holocaust).

Twenty years later, with actor Harrison Ford twenty years older, the third sequel, *Indiana Jones and the Kingdom of the Crystal Skull*, was set in the 1950s. There weren't enough Nazis anymore to be the hero's great enemy, so the villain was a communist Russian. Australian actress Cate Blanchett apologised to Russians for her character, as I never heard any actor or actress apologise to Germans for Nazi villains.

Mel Brooks, an American Jew born Melvin Kaminsky, said he thought the best way to keep Nazism from ever reviving was by laughing at it. The audience in his 1968 film *The Producers*, like the audience watching the film, was at first offended by dancing Nazis singing "It's springtime for Hitler and Germany, it's winter for Poland and France." As the Germans became more stupid, both audiences learned to laugh.

Among a miscellany of villainy, Nazis also appeared in Brooks' 1974 film *Blazing Saddles*. Brilliant as he was with films like *High Anxiety* and television series like *Get Smart*, to paraphrase an observation from one of the humorous books I bought through my university years, Brooks was totally obsessed about Nazis.

The Western film genre generally celebrated the honour and heroism of the frontiersmen and women who built America, but

Blazing Saddles turned history upside down. In Brooks' telling, those ordinary white people who built America became frightened morons. The hero was a charming smart Negro, who a lisping German beauty (played by Jewess Madeline Kahn) sought to seduce and abandon, thereby breaking him, until she fell in love with him. Most characters in the film did.

Playing the greatest of all gunslingers was Jewish actor Gene Wilder. "They've smashed racism in the face," remarked Wilder of the film, "but they're doing it while you laugh."

Also mocking racists was Jewish writer Johnny Speight with the television series *Till Death Us Do Part*, which began in 1965. Not everyone understood the satire. Jewish actor Warren Mitchell (born Warren Misell), told the story of a fan of the show who congratulated him for denigrating black immigrants with his portrayal of Alf Garnett (who inspired Archie Bunker in the equivalent American series *All in the Family*). Mitchell replied that the show and character denigrated people like the fan.

Jewish actor Henry Winkler was so charming and charismatic a star I saw the 1977 film *Heroes* because he was in it. He'd become a cult hero playing the leather-jacketed, motorcycle-riding Fonz, Arthur Fonzarelli, in the nostalgic American television series *Happy Days*, which premiered in 1974. A fictitious look back to a time, the 1950s, that no longer was became one that never had been when likeable characters confronted the racism of unlikeable others in the episodes 'The Best Man' and 'Fonzie's New Friend,' written by Joel Kane and by Sid Arthur and Artie Laing respectively. When the normally über cool Fonz saw a sign saying a bar was for white people only, he seized up with disgust. He made racism uncool.

Happy Days became science fiction with the appearance of an unidentified flying object and Mork from the planet Ork. Mork went onto get his own television series, with a kind woman named Mindy. Ed Scharlach and Tom Tenowich wrote the *Mork & Mindy* episode 'The Night They Raided Mind-ski's', in which white people wanting to clean up Boulder, Colorado slowly revealed their racism. Mindy lectured Mork (and the audience) about the evils they represented.

With his alien powers, Mork thus changed their skin to a myriad of colours and patterns, as if human races were just colours of skin. The studio audience (real or contrived) enthusiastically applauded, humiliating those racists. Watching from our homes, we could hardly help but be caught up in the revelry.

Germans were the focus of the American television series *Hogan's Heroes*, premiering in 1965. At the time, it was the only television comedy about Nazis, but these were blundering oafs running the Stalag 13 prisoner-of-war camp frightened of the *Schutzstaffel* storm troopers, Gestapo secret police, and being sent to the gruesome Eastern Front. The series separated Germans into menacing black-shirts we feared and cowardly fools we treated with contempt. Mocking them thinking they were a master race, nobody needed to mention anything so distasteful as race or racism for audiences to know.

Far from fighting a war, they were nevertheless part of a war machine. The jokes at which we laughed and escapes of Allied prisoners of war we cheered didn't allow us time to pause and think about it, but the show quietly made all Germans complicit in the war. German bank managers and toymakers who became seemingly harmless camp commandants and guards were complicit in the Holocaust

Perhaps so I could survive another war against the only enemy I imagined, I studied the German language through my first four years of high school. In third and fourth form, including four weeks of reading a classic German novel at the end of fourth form, my auburn-haired teacher was a man my small-boy memories recall as being more Scottish than anything else, but perhaps everything about the school seemed Scottish. None of my German-language teachers was German.

One day, among the lighter moments maturing boys could make becoming a little less scared of our teachers, a classroom conversation turned to *Hogan's Heroes*. Henderson's manner became uncommonly stern. In response to a show at which I'd only laughed, he called it a slander against the German people.

A slander against Jews would be anti-Semitism. There was no word for slanders against Germans. There still isn't.

The slanders so wrong were by European peoples. We'd committed the Holocaust. Other races hadn't.

Playing Frenchman Corporal Lebeau in *Hogan's Heroes* was a French Jew formerly imprisoned at Buchenwald, Robert Clary, who estimated that fourteen members of his immediate family died in the Holocaust. "They were not killed," he said of the French prisoners of war. "They were not sent to gas chambers."

We didn't know it then, and wouldn't have thought about it if we had, but all the regular German characters on *Hogan's Heroes* were played by Jews. Howard Caine played the cruel Major Hochstetter of the Gestapo. Leon Askin, who was beaten by the Gestapo and spent the Second World War in a French internment camp, played General Burkhalter. Werner Klemperer only agreed to play Colonel Klink on condition that Klink's schemes always failed.

The further down in rank the nicer and stupider the German characters became (much as poorer Britons, Americans, and Australians did in other television series). Austrian Jew John Banner played fat Sergeant Schultz. Three decades later, the finance director of Holyman Limited still mimicked him, exclaiming in his best faux-German accent, "I know nothing!"

In Jewish writer Woody Allen's 2016 film *Café Society*, Veronica Hayes told Jewish nightclub manager Bobby Dorfman that she liked Jews because they were exotic. He promptly sought to bed her. "It's true what they say," she told him, "you people are pushy."

Bobby's brother Ben was a murderer. At the end of the film, shortly before his execution, Ben became a Christian. "First a murderer," laments their mother, "then he becomes a Christian. What did I do to deserve this? Which is worse?" Their father said Ben's pending death led to his conversion. "We are all afraid of dying, Marty, but we don't give up the religion we are born into."

When German model Heidi Klum arrived at the annual Elton John AIDS Foundation party in 2013 wearing a dress to reveal much of her beautiful backside, American Jewish comedienne Joan Rivers saw the chance for a joke. Speaking on her *Fashion Police* show, Rivers remarked, "The last time a German looked this hot was when they were pushing Jews into the ovens."

Abraham Foxman from the Anti-Defamation League wasn't concerned about the insult to Germans. He called her comment "vulgar and offensive to Jews and Holocaust survivors."

Rivers refused to apologise. "My husband lost the majority of his family at Auschwitz," she said, "and I can assure you that I have always made it a point to remind people of the Holocaust through humour."

A year earlier, American retailer Costco refused to sell Rivers' book, *I Hate Everything... Starting With Me*, for which she accused the store of being like Nazi Germany. "Germany is where banning books started, and it can start here just as quickly."

7. GERMAN IDENTITY

Nationalism grew through nineteenth-century Europe from a need for peace and security. Napoleon and the French military threat motivated Germanic states to confederate in 1814 and eventually unify in 1871. The German people's long tolerance of Jews made Jews numerous there, although unification was without Austria for the efforts of Otto von Bismarck, for whom Prussian nationalism mattered more than German nationalism. Liberation from the French and Austrians were among the motives gradually melding Italian city states into Italy.

To my French friend Patrick reading Carl von Clausewitz' classic treatise *On War*, I'm indebted for the knowledge that Prussian and other soldiers had more to fear from their officers than their enemies. Soldiers were often mercenaries fighting for plunder before nationalism gave them reason to defend their compatriots. Nationalism protected people not as strong as the strongest, not as rich as the richest. Nationalism was virtuous.

That was before our two world wars and the Jewish Holocaust of the twentieth century. Gustav Heinemann, president of the Federal Republic of Germany, told his fellow Germans in 1969, "I don't love the state," their country. He at least went onto say, "I love my wife." They had four children.

There'd been no celebrating so unloved a nation on her twentieth birthday, but I learned of the Heinemann quote on her sixtieth birthday, with optimism things were improving. Germans were reportedly learning more of their history than the Holocaust, but were still building memorials to victims of long-dead Germans at war: at that time gypsies and homosexuals. Things didn't improve.

"I think young Germans and young Israelis share a lot in common," said Naor Narkis, a young Israeli, in 2014. "We both grew up in the shadow of the Holocaust, and in that sense, we understand each other." He advocated Israelis moving to Berlin, where "you find the lowest level of anti-Semitism in Europe," to live cheaper than in Israel. "I was always curious about Germany, because I wanted to understand a society that almost exterminated my people..., and I also love my country, Israel."

A Monday in September 1986, my girlfriend and I sat aboard a train travelling from Rennes to Chartres in France. With us in the compartment, as they were with us each day, were our backpacks. Also with us that day was a seventeen-year-old German boy from a town thirty kilometres outside Munich. "I am at the *Gymnasium*?" he said, uncertain of the English word he should use.

"The school?" I asked.

"Yes."

His father was an engineer, his mother kept home, and his two sisters were also at school. He'd cycled to St Malo on the Brittany coast, but was returning home by train. We talked about Europe and about Germany. "Are you worried about the low birth rate in Germany?" I asked him.

"No."

"But what if all the Germans were to die out?"

"So? It wouldn't matter."

"Why not?"

"Because of what we've done."

"Do you mean the war?" I asked. World War II had ended more than forty years earlier.

"Not the war, that was just a war, but what we did to the Jews." Other victims, least of all Germans, weren't in his thoughts.

Dutch, French, and other collaborators who assisted and let happen the Holocaust didn't diminish his sense of culpability. My father believed the Dutch contributed several divisions to fight for Nazi Germany. Dutch Nazis were reputedly more dangerous than German Nazis because, without years of propaganda characterising Jews by their stooped shoulders, hooked noses, and menacing stares, the Dutch could better spot real Jews. Hungary had developed anti-Semitic laws of her own and, after initially hoping to keep out of the war, formally joined the Axis with Germany and Italy in 1940.

"That was also a war," I told him, "and besides you weren't there."

"I know, but I am still German." Standing convicted of their racial guilt, Germans punish themselves.

"What about all the great achievements of the Germans?" I

asked him. "Beethoven?"

He shrugged his shoulders. I could've sat with him for a day listing great German composers, writers, film-makers, and thinkers, and he would have still shrugged his shoulders. I could have sat with him for a week listing German scientific, intellectual, and technological accomplishments without getting his attention. Nazism was an anomaly in German and Western history, but those twelve years had become Germany's only history.

"Look at every country," I told him. "Look what my country did in the Boer War." Australian and New Zealand soldiers first fought in the Second Boer War, from 1899 to 1902, with other British. We converted independent Boer republics into British colonies, scorched the earth, and invented concentration camps. "We killed people I wished we hadn't, but I'm not taking the blame. The Germans weren't the only people to kill Jews." I was thinking of the Russian pogroms, but other people also killed Jews. "I think it would be a shame for any group to disappear," I told him. "It's not fair that Germans are the only ones not allowed to care for themselves."

A few weeks after meeting the young German, my girlfriend and I were in Vienna. Walking alone through the dark streets after an argument between us, I came upon a graphic statue of a man in chains stepping through blocks of rock. Terror bound the figure, to spite the last resilience in his weary eyes and steps. The Holocaust memorial demanded *"Niemals Vergessen."* Never forget.

Instead of keeping their past misdeeds to the peripheries, Austrians and Germans build monuments to theirs in town and city centres. The following month, amidst the Sunday afternoon strollers in little Göttingen, I walked upon a shining column of aluminium Stars of David twisted above a hole, immortalising the site of a synagogue destroyed on *Kristallnacht*, 1938.

In our fight against our white racist past, we have no greater force than post-Holocaust Germany. Germans are at odds with their parents and grandparents. Veterans are at odds with themselves. It's their war of liberation against a totalitarian dictatorship, but one in which they've taken responsibility as no other race on earth takes for its dictators. It's their chance to join the rest of the West against a common foe: that moment in history when their people traditionally among the most tolerant of Jews were never less tolerant.

Germany was partitioned after the Second World War, with the Federal Republic of Germany, democratic West Germany, quick to apologise for the Holocaust and pay reparations. The German Democratic Republic, communist East Germany, didn't. Communists rejected racial guilt to say that only the Nazis were responsible; communists had fought against Nazis. Only with the coming of democracy in 1990 did East Germany apologise for the genocide of "*the Jews in all European countries, the people of the Soviet Union, the Polish people and the Gypsy people.*"

Jews received an extra apology. East European communists condemned racism and anti-Semitism, but hadn't embraced Jews after the Holocaust as had West Europeans. "*We ask the people of Israel to forgive us for the hypocrisy and hostility of official East German policies toward Israel and for the persecution and degradation of Jewish citizens also after 1945 in our country.*" German racial guilt encompassed explicit Nazi anti-Semitism and subtler communist anti-Semitism. (We've forgotten communist anti-Semitism.)

Other European countries embraced German guilt as their own. In 1995, President Jacques Chirac apologised for France's role in the Holocaust. My eldest son's studies of modern history in his last year of school taught him that Vichy France enacted anti-Semitic laws exceeding those instructed by Germany.

On International Holocaust Remembrance Day 2012, Prime Minister Jens Stoltenberg apologised that Norwegians had deported Jews to their deaths. "Norway acted similarly to Vichy France in that they implemented their own anti-Jewish laws, used their own manpower, confiscated property, and discriminated against Jews before the Germans had demanded it," said historian Paul Levine at Uppsala University, Sweden. "Norway didn't have to do what it did."

The crime we made Germany's in the aftermath of the war became their crime, too. Germany's racial guilt became their racial guilt.

To this day, white people knowing only one aspect of World War II know that Germany murdered six million Jews. We know nothing else about Nazis, their policies, or actions. We don't wonder why they killed Jews. We're not conscious that sixty million other people died through the war. Up to six million Russians, Poles, Yugoslavs, and others also died in the Holocaust.

We're fixated with the wrongs European peoples committed

against other races. We're not so interested about those we committed against each other.

For all our apologies to Jews, we don't apologise to Germans for the massive land seizures and cruel reparations that we (especially France) imposed upon Germany after World War I. Germany invaded the Polish Corridor dividing Germany from Danzig in 1939 to bring those Germanic regions back into Germany; I've heard said that Hitler ordered the consumption of Czechoslovakia before the invasion of the Polish Corridor because he knew Germany's claim to the Polish Corridor was much stronger than any claim to Czechoslovakia. In all our contemplations that other people's misconduct might be due to our past misdeeds, we don't contemplate our role in humiliating Germany in the 1919 Treaty of Versailles for the rise of Nazism.

In an article titled 'Shall we All commit Suicide?' published in *Pall Mall Magazine* in September 1924, Winston Churchill wrote of the risk of war returning to Europe. One reason was Russia, the Soviet Union, bemoaning the loss of *"her Baltic Provinces."* The other was Germany's bitterness towards France.

"From one end of Germany to the other an intense hatred of France unites the whole population," wrote Churchill. *"The enormous contingents of German youth growing to military manhood year by year are inspired by the fiercest sentiments, and the soul of Germany smoulders with dreams of a War of Liberation or Revenge. These ideas are restrained at the present moment only by physical impotence."*

Nor do we apologise for Germany's land forfeitures and other suffering immediately after World War II. Everybody lost that war. Germany lost most. Sydney's Cardinal George Pell has been among those to observe that no people have been punished as Germans have been punished for the Holocaust.

The only apologies we don't make are to white people. They don't warrant our apology.

Five years after sitting with that young German in a train in France, I was again in Europe with a backpack beside me. By then, the summer of 1991, Germany was reunited. This time, I too was alone. Sitting with me in a carriage on a train from Frankfurt to Munich was another German, a much older man. At fifty or more years of age, I'd have called him old that only time we met, but he no longer seems old. He'd lived through the Second World War but been too young to fight.

The train stopped at Ulm, when perhaps the conversation between us started, or perhaps that was when the conversation between us became personal. I don't know why it should have been at Ulm. The man told me he'd lived in the Sudetenland until the Czechoslovakian government evicted him and other ethnic Germans after the war. He was careful to say that Czechs, not simply communists or even Slovakians, evicted them.

The evictions weren't political. They were racial. Those German men, women, and children were evicted without thought as to who were Nazis. They were evicted for being German.

He spoke of discrimination with the sorrow of the dispossessed and the anger of the victim tired of being the accused. I'd never before thought of the Germans who'd lived in the Sudetenland, not even when my high school history classes spoke of Nazi Germany subsuming it without war from Czechoslovakia in 1938. Nor had I heard of the ethnic Germans forced back into broken Germany after the war. They were a dispossessed, I've never heard mentioned again.

That frightened small boy had become a sorrowed aged man, lost among the guilty people of whom the young German with a bicycle had spoken five years earlier in another, distant train. The aged man condemned nationalism but lauded patriotism, in a distinction new to me.

Nationalism and patriotism had been one through my lifetime. My schoolboy history classes and other public history blamed the First World War on European nationalism and the Second on German nationalism, bundling racism into the nationalistic wrong.

On the train from Ulm, I slowly understood. We could love our people, country, and selves without harming others. Patriots cared for their people, loving their countries, even if they're too fearful to mention it beyond their closest confidants and solitary Australians on trains willing to listen.

Of all the suffering in the world of which I've heard so much, the suffering of which I've heard least has been Europe's. The least of the least has been Germany's.

A similar number of Germans as Jews died in World War II. They amounted to more than ten percent of the German population.

We presume all Germans participated in the Holocaust, although only a tiny proportion did. At its peak, no more than ten percent of the German population were members of the Nazi Party, doubtlessly including many joining for the sake of their careers in a totalitarian state. They weren't the same ten percent who died.

My Polish acquaintance Ryk's sister spent four years in the Auschwitz concentration camp. She told him German guards were kind, especially to children. They acknowledged the craziness they couldn't stop.

Eric Khan was the middle of three sons of a Jewish family in Nazi Germany. He survived the Holocaust because a German family sheltered him as its own.

Eric would live to be an old man, leaving behind a widow, Margaret, who my wife befriended. She said many German Jews survived the Holocaust because networks of Germans risked their lives to save them.

Germans treated our soldiers and prisoners according to the Geneva Conventions of war. Throughout their occupation of Paris, they allowed French Great War veterans to continue lighting a flame above France's Tomb of the Unknown Soldier at six thirty each night.

Our parish Anglican priest Father Keith, a former submariner, told me Adolf Hitler ordered German soldiers to respect all war memorials. The only war memorial the Nazis destroyed was one portraying a German soldier being killed in the Great War. Two German soldiers caught urinating on a British war memorial were offered the choice between committing suicide and serving on the Russian Front. They chose the latter.

In September 1942, a German U-boat fired upon and sank the Royal Mail Ship *Laconia*, believing her to be carrying British troops, but the sight and cries of drowning passengers told Captain Werner Hartenstein the ship had been carrying Italian prisoners of war, Polish guards, and British women and children. He began rescuing them under the Red Cross flag, while other German U-boats came to assist. They saved hundreds before an American B-24 Liberator bombed them. Of necessity, Admiral Karl Dönitz subsequently ordered German submarines not to attempt rescuing survivors from downed ships.

None of it still matters. Germany's remorse to the Jews didn't have to affect her relations with other races, but she responded to the Holocaust in her treatment of not just Jews but herself. If the

Holocaust made Jewish identity fundamentally one of being a victim determined never to be a victim again, then it led to a German identity of being a criminal struggling to be anything else. If Germans and other European peoples taking aboard guilt for the Holocaust aren't to be goose-stepping, genocidal racists, then we'd better be diehard opponents of our race. Our sense of ourselves became our deference to others.

8. IMPERIAL TURKEY

The second Wednesday in May, 2012, my middle-born daughter observed a large group of Asian students clustered together at school. "That's a lot of Asians," she remarked.

"Racist!" a Turkish friend chided her.

My daughter didn't understand; she'd meant nothing more than to observe. The following morning, she asked me if her words were racist.

"Yes," I replied.

"Oops."

To be racist no longer requires discrimination or judgement. Any recognition of race, or sense races exist, has become racist.

We needn't even be mentioning people for talk to turn to racism. "If you leave cupcakes too long in the oven," my daughter remarked, in a conversation in the kitchen of a friend's home, "they'll go black."

"Racist!" said her Turkish friend.

Racism is for the West. Other races aren't shy.

"My family calls Abos 'niggers'," said the same friend, in another conversation with my daughter. Being Turkish, she was Muslim. "My family hates yours," she told my daughter without malice, "for being Christians."

The Turks are an Asian race, retaining privilege in the country, Turkey, they took from the Greeks in 1453, less than seventy years before Spain conquered the Aztec Empire and only a century and a half before British settlement of the Americas began. Turks invaded their way into Europe and have never completely been evicted, but most races have enjoyed choosing the lands they occupy and incurred others making choices for them. To their credit and good sense, the Turks with whom I shared cold tea in 1993 in Istanbul valued being Turkish.

Among the punishments imposed upon their portions of a partitioned Germany after World War II, the victorious American, British, and French occupying forces imposed laws compelling

Germany to accept immigrants from other races and religions. The new Federal Republic of Germany was open not just to Jews, but to everyone. There was no pretence then that racial and religious diversity would make Germany strong. We came up with that half a century later, after other Western countries opened our borders to all comers too.

The most numerous to come to Germany were the Turks, but the guilt dogging Germans isn't one they besmirch upon their innocent immigrants. We deem those immigrants to be German by their residency if not their citizenship, except in matters of guilt. Their race exonerates them.

The only seat I could get when I boarded a crowded train coming home from Town Hall station the third Tuesday evening in September 2010 was between two other people. By the window was a woman not quite as old as I was, with sandy brown hair and not so much tan in her skin as to wrinkle it. There wasn't any reason to notice her (any more than there was reason to notice the East Asian woman adjoining the aisle talking on her telephone, before alighting) until the woman by the window leant forward, reached her hand over the top of the seat, and touched the back of the man's head sitting in front of me.

Sydneysiders had stopped talking to each other on trains since we'd become individualistic, multiracial. We'd stopped leaning forward and touching the back of people's heads sitting in front of us. I leant a little forward to look.

"There was a bug on his collar," the woman explained. "He must think I'm mad."

With the wires from two small speakers hanging from his ears, he hadn't noticed her at all. "That was really good of you," I told her.

"I'd want someone doing that for me."

"I know, but most people don't think like that. They're too self-absorbed."

"It depends on where you are."

"It's like that in Sydney."

"It is, isn't it? I suppose it's just having a social conscience."

"Most people's idea of a social conscience is transferring money to people they've never met."

She leant forward again. "There it is," she said.

I saw a little black insect crawling on the man's shirt. She again brushed it away. The man reached his hand back and adjusted his collar.

"What's he thinking about me?" she asked me.

"He's not even thinking about you."

We continued to talk. I learnt she was German, although she'd left Germany many years earlier. I mentioned having been there, to which she replied, "It's hard when you don't know the language."

"I don't speak Turkish."

She smiled. "Do you know *Der Zeil*, the main shopping street in Frankfurt?"

I shook my head.

"I was the most German person there," she told me, before smiling. "Hitler must be turning in his grave."

Not just her words but her attitude, a sense of glorious revenge against a dictator dead before she was born, stunned me. It didn't matter, nor even occur to me at the time, that Adolf Hitler had no grave, unless she meant the West. She celebrated Germany becoming home to other races: an act of vengeful derision.

"I like it that Germany is so diverse," she said, by which she meant other races growing so much.

"I like Germany," I told her. "Toy shops in…," I started to say, but I checked myself before mentioning Nuremberg, "old towns, old clocks, forests, fairy tales."

"A lot of bad things happen in fairy tales."

Not only Jews died in the Holocaust, so did the Brothers Grimm. People who'd produced stories such as Cinderella and Sleeping Beauty no longer wanted fairy tales.

Neither does the rest of the West. We live fairy tales nevertheless, without knowing they are.

A year earlier, the Anzac commemoration service programme at our parish Anglican church included an image of an enemy Turkish soldier waving a white flag to help a wounded British soldier in the first Anzac campaign, 1915. That single Turkish soldier would again be mentioned at Remembrance Sunday 2014. Three million soldiers fought for the Ottoman Empire in the Great War alone, but we made that one man representative of all Turkish soldiers in our new-found conviction their soldiers were as noble as ours, if not nobler.

In 1915, a fifth of Turkey's population was Christian. So might that good soldier have been.

Australian war remembrance services fashionably mourn enemies past, other than Nazis, as the equals of our soldiers. Anything else would be discriminatory.

Talking to Vietnam War veteran C.J. Smith at lunch after the 2009 Anzac service taught me several things, such as how much we both liked devilled eggs. A tall sturdy man, his white hair seemed incongruous to his build and gait. He'd made ninety-four trips overseas, trying to travel all the great rivers, visit all the great civilisations, and be everywhere there stood an Australian war memorial.

C.J. said all the religions on earth imposed their beliefs upon others except Buddhism. (Buddhists are too self-absorbed to bother.) In fact, as he slowly agreed, only two traditional religions had: Christianity and Islam. We didn't really impose Christianity, but until the Holocaust we taught it to be the religion for every man, woman, and child on earth. The Koran requires Muslims to convert non-believers.

After meeting an Armenian tending to the Church of the Holy Sepulchre in Jerusalem, C.J. visited Armenia. Armenians are a proud people: proud to have been the first Christian nation, proud of their culture, proud of much more. The day before that first Anzac Day, the twenty-fifth of April 1915, when ninety-four years later we spoke of our noble past-enemy, those same Turks began their massacre of two million Christian Armenians. Turks didn't value life as we did, in spite of the pictures in our parish Anglican church programmes almost a century later.

Armenians honour their people and civilisation, as we so pitifully fail to honour ours. They didn't lose faith as the Jews and we lost faith. They have retained their sense of being a people and nation.

In Armenia, their land, they planted two million trees around a concrete spire reaching to heaven, much as our cathedrals once did. In a huge, thick-walled concrete structure C.J. described as being like half an orange cut into segments, the spaces between segments allowed visitors to enter and stand obscured from the world outside, but for a large hole in the roof. In the ground were planted and cut two million short roses, whose aroma breathed through the memorial. I asked C.J. for a word to describe his senses there. He said there wasn't a word.

In the West, we no longer build memorials for our people. That would be nationalistic, insensitive. We build them for everyone else.

Turks in Turkey, Germany, and everywhere else feel no shame for the atrocities of their racial past. Article 301 of the Turkish Penal Code prohibited insulting *"Turkishness"* until 2008, since which time it's prohibited insulting *"the Turkish Nation."* Both forbid talk of the Armenian Genocide. Acknowledging only there were deportations, some Armenians starved, or that criminal acts by Armenian gangs necessitated their killing, Turkey prohibits people from saying the Armenian Genocide occurred.

Conversely, Germany, Austria, and other European countries prohibit people from saying the Jewish Holocaust didn't occur, or trivialising it by questioning the numbers of Jews killed. Exact casualty figures are often unknowable, but five to six million dead is the most widely accepted estimate. I wish it had been less, and would have thought suggestions of lesser figures would console, not offend. I wish all the casualty figures I cite had been less.

We don't say much about the Armenian Genocide, either; I don't recall any film or television programme mentioning it. Under pressure from Turkey, the American Congress deferred consideration of an Armenian Genocide Resolution finally introduced on the penultimate day of January 2007.

The Armenian Genocide hasn't led to the same revulsion against Muslims or Turks that the Jewish Holocaust has created against Christians, Germans, and other European peoples. It hasn't led to a revulsion against anything. Perhaps not enough Armenians make films and television series.

"Who after all is today speaking about the destruction of the Armenians?" reportedly asked Hitler, in his speech at Obersalzberg a week before Germany invaded Poland in 1939.

Germany post Holocaust is. While Turkey denies that there was an Armenian Genocide, Germany, being Germany, takes responsibility for the genocide.

In April 2015, German president Joachim Gauck attended a religious service in Berlin commemorating the centenary of the start of the Armenian Genocide. He said the German Empire bore "shared responsibility, possibly shared guilt for the genocide," for having been Ottoman Turkey's ally in the Great War and deploying soldiers who took part in "planning and, in part, carrying out the deportations."

In 2018 in Cologne, by the Rhine River and Hohenzollern Bridge near the famous cathedral, Germany erected a memorial to the victims of the Armenian Genocide. Headed "*This pain affects us all*" in English and German, the memorial blamed the "*Ottoman Empire and allied German generals, under the command of Emperor Willhelm II.*"

The Cologne memorial alluded to the Jewish Holocaust in World War II being the reason the West rejected racial and religious discrimination and refused to examine race and religion in any way such that people might rank one as better than another, however awful people of other races and religions might be. "*Similar crimes can only be prevented by steadfastly rejecting the discrimination of minorities and by acknowledging that no religion, nationality, or ethnicity is superior to another,*" said the memorial.

In spite of having committed the Armenian genocide, Turks came to enjoy immunity from racial or religious scrutiny in the West. Everyone did, except us. We prefer to suffer other races and religions in ignorance than to risk other races and religions suffering at our hands.

Nor do Turks put up with anyone mentioning their massacres of hundreds of thousands of Christian Assyrians during and after World War I. In our struggle to manage other people's racial tensions, Fairfield City Council approved the Assyrian Universal Alliance's request to build a monument in Bonnyrigg, suburban Sydney to the massacres on condition it didn't blame anyone for them. Thus the plaque on the front of the memorial, unveiled in August 2010, read, "*This memorial is dedicated to the victims of the Assyrian genocide (Seyfo) in WW1 1914-1918, Simele massacre 1933 and onwards.*" It was like remembering victims of the Jewish Holocaust without mentioning Nazis.

The problem for the people of Fairfield was a second plaque, which Hermiz Shahen explained was an "informational note" attached for just a few hours after unveiling to give the sculpture some historical background. "*During WW1 (1914-1918) they were exposed to the worst kind of extermination and genocide by the Ottoman Turks.*"

The Turkish consul general to Sydney, Renan Sekeroglu, was furious, saying the note "angered and disillusioned the one hundred and fifty thousand Turkish Australians." Australian citizenship didn't keep them from being his constituency: Turks of the Turkish

Nation.

Other races don't share our passion for guilt. They retain their loyalties, respecting and defending their generations dead before they were born.

Quietly, a few of us know the Armenian Genocide occurred, although I'd never heard of the Assyrian Genocide until I read the report of Turks complaining about the Bonnyrigg memorial. I'd not even known any Assyrians were left in the world, presuming they'd died out in ancient times as they nearly died out at the hands of the Turks only a century ago.

I had not known until I was writing this book that on the fourteenth day of November 1914, the Caliph of the Ottoman Empire declared a Holy War against infidels: Christians. From 1913 until '23, the Turks also carried out their Greek Genocide, killing as many as nine hundred thousand Greeks and destroying much of our Christian and classic European heritage.

Turks were never punished for their Christian Holocausts. Crimes by other races don't consume us; we don't dwell upon their atrocities. We don't make Turkish perpetrators of genocide representative of Turks or Muslims everywhere, then or now, as we make German perpetrators representative of Germans and Christians then, now, and always. Jews and we keep punishing Germany and the West, our subsequent generations.

Through it all, the Jewish Holocaust retains a special status. Not just the archetypal genocide it is, for us, the only genocide: the best known killing in history. The Friday after school at the end of his first full week of year six, my second son asked me if "what Hitler did" was the worst of crimes. He'd never heard of communist tyrants Joseph Stalin or Mao Zedong.

Among the ghoul galleries, Stalin and Mao wilfully killed many more people, but Hitler may well have proven to be the single most destructive person in history. All genocides shape their victims, but no other affects the perpetrators as the Jewish Holocaust cuts a swathe through the West, denying us the chance to be what other races remain. Without it, we'd still consider racial and religious loyalty virtues, as other races do. Rather than individual self-interest or narrow minded regionalism, we'd speak up for broad-minded nationalism expressed with a desire to keep out of war, as we did through the 1930s. We'd honour our dead we've come to dismiss.

The Jewish Holocaust gave rise to a narrative that the worst forces for oppression and war through history have been Christian Western prejudice: that we've been forever cruel to other races and religions. We espouse a falsified history by which we're long-guilty wrongdoers and other races our long-suffering victims, editing history to exonerate everyone else. Other races have bought into it as if it were true. The innocence of Jews through the Holocaust is the innocence of non-Europeans forever. Sometime, surely, it can stop.

9. IMPERIAL JAPAN

Hanging from a thick stone wall of the nineteenth-century chapel in our parish Anglican church is a wooden cross from Malaya, dated the day after Australia Day 1942, brought home by Australian soldiers honouring their fallen comrades. Above it hang military banners their colours fading, which older people keep from rotting. I'm not sure most parishioners pay much attention anymore.

Our forebears were other people; we're not interested in other people's wars. War in Asia is yesterday's news, wars against other countries anachronistic. We don't fight other races. That would be racist.

It was all very different the first Sunday of December 1941, when Imperial Japan attacked American Hawaii. "Men and women of Australia," said Prime Minister John Curtain in a radio address that day. "We are at war with Japan. This is the gravest hour of our history. We Australians have imperishable traditions. We shall maintain them. We shall vindicate them. We shall hold this country and keep it as a citadel for the British-speaking race and as a place where civilisation will persist."

World War II was an Asian war before it became a world war, but Imperial Japan was hardly the product of Western prejudice, however much Japan mimicked Europe. Almost unknown to the West today was Japan occupying Manchuria from 1931, invading the rest of China in 1937, and thereafter expanding across Asia and the Pacific towards Australia. While Adolf Hitler became the most infamous figure on earth, few of us today could name Japan's wartime emperor, Hirohito.

Estimates vary widely, but Japanese murdered most likely from three to ten million civilians, including seven million Chinese, from 1931 to '45. (American historian Chalmers Johnson estimated the number at thirty million, including twenty-three million Chinese.) In the Rape of Nanking, Japanese soldiers raped and murdered three hundred thousand Chinese civilians and unarmed soldiers through six weeks in 1937.

Army surgeon Shiro Ishii and his secret Unit 731 experimented upon as many as twelve thousand non-Japanese, including Western prisoners of war. They vivisected young women in the Philippines to teach soldiers about female anatomy, infected prisoners with diseases such as syphilis, and studied living people freezing in extreme cold and crumpling under extreme pressure. A six-foot-tall white man was cut into two and preserved in a large vial of formaldehyde.

What once were facts we all knew, or at least some of us knew, became yesterday's secrets. Japanese soldiers enslaved something like two hundred thousand Western and Asian women, beating and raping them as they willed. When we make a rare mention of it, we dehumanise the women. They're the "comfort women," a delightfully inoffensive phrase making them sound like fluffy cushions on a sofa rather than sex slaves tied to Japanese beds.

War is horrible. For us, the most horrific horrors through World War II didn't come from Germany. Ours were European conventions of compassion and respect, not shared by the Japanese. When Hong Kong fell, the Japanese slaughtered British medical staff. Twenty-one Australian Army nurses reached Bangka Island after their ship was bombed and sunk, only to be massacred by Japanese.

My friend Don's mother's first husband was among the Australian soldiers killed and eaten by Japanese soldiers in New Guinea, while rice remained uneaten. Consequently, Australian soldiers there didn't take any Japanese prisoners of war.

Graeme, at my Baptist church and a former research assistant in the School of Physics at Sydney University, told me in 2015 that America's General Douglas Macarthur refused to award Australian soldiers citations after a successful campaign because he thought we'd breached the Geneva conventions of war by not taking Japanese prisoners. Graeme was unaware of the reason.

Japan ordered that no captured soldier should survive the war. Japanese captors forced their prisoners of war into slave labour, giving them little, if any, food or medical attention.

Japan enslaved twelve thousand American prisoners of war to work for the Japanese government and Japanese companies, of whom eleven hundred died. Political and commercial expediency led Mitsubishi Materials Corporation, on behalf of its predecessor

Mitsubishi Mining Company, to become the first major Japanese company to apologise for those actions, at a special ceremony at a Los Angeles museum in 2015. Until then, I'd never heard of that enslavement and murder.

In 1942, Japanese soldiers set upwards of sixty thousand Filipino and American prisoners of war on the Bataan Death March. As many as ten thousand Filipinos and six hundred and fifty Americans died.

As well as the infamous Burma Railway, the Japanese forced prisoners of war and slave labourers to build a military airstrip at Sandakan, Borneo. Most Australian and British prisoners of war and Indonesian slave labourers were already dead by early 1945, when Allied landings nearby led the camp commandant to march the last prisoners to another camp, two hundred and fifty kilometres away. Eighteen hundred Australian and seven hundred and thirty-eight British prisoners of war died. The only survivors were six servicemen who escaped.

We forgave. Among the dead in the Sandakan Death March was Ted Dunhill. A generation or two onward, the Dunhill family of Boonderoo donated limestone rocks for the Japanese Garden in the New South Wales town of Cowra. The town made heroes of the Japanese who tried to escape their prisoner-of-war camp in 1944, in spite of them killing five Australians. During my visit to the Cowra Visitor Information Centre with three of my children in 2012, the story of an Australian veteran befriending a former Japanese soldier meant to inspire us further to embrace our past enemy Japan, as we don't embrace Germany.

We forgot. My father, the mayor of the Ku-ring-gai Municipality in 1989, knew nothing of Sandakan until a resident told him about it. He'd been one of those six survivors.

However little we care about history when we were victims, we're positively hostile to history when the people harming us weren't Western. Ku-ring-gai Municipal Council resolved to establish what would be the first memorial in Australia to the Sandakan victims, but the Australian government was furious. Wanting not to offend Japan, it pressed the council not to proceed, although the memorial would be no more than a small brass plaque on a broken sandstone column, in a quiet suburban street. My father sent the government a copy of the proposed inscription, saying the council would correct anything factually inaccurate, but the government wasn't contesting the facts. It was trying to prevent anyone mentioning them

Nothing's changed. For fear of upsetting Japan, the Department of Defence advised the Australian government in 2008 not to mention the World War II sinking of the Australian hospital ship *Centaur*, in which two hundred and sixty medical personnel and civilian crew died. *"There is a strong reticence in Japan to engage on wartime issues,"* pointed out the report signed on the first Thursday of September 2008 by Peter West, an assistant secretary of the department's International Policy Division and endorsed by the Departments of Foreign Affairs and Trade and of Prime Minister and Cabinet. *"We want to avoid a public debate over whether the sinking of the Australian Hospital Ship Centaur was legal."*

There was hardly a cause for debate. The sinking was plainly illegal by Western conventions, but Japan never accepted responsibility for an attack that Prime Minister John Curtin at the time said violated "all the principles of common humanity."

He was naïve. There is no common humanity. Somebody once told me that, after the war, the Japanese deliberately sent prostitutes carrying venereal disease to meet American soldiers occupying Japan.

Through his fourth year of high school, my youngest son's history teacher admitted that the Japanese committed atrocities during World War II. The truth being politically unacceptable, the teacher read a statement from the New South Wales Department of Education that there was fault on both sides: that Australians committed atrocities against the Japanese and the Japanese committed them against Australians.

The statement was untrue. It was also a gross insult to our forebears who fought, suffered, and died in our defence.

As I pointed out to my son, telling me about it soon afterwards, no such statement ever accompanied criticisms of white people. No statement about the Holocaust accused the Jews of genocide against Germans.

While Jews spoke so much about the Holocaust, our traumatised soldiers trying to come home from the war said little about Japan. The victorious Allies tried individual Japanese, but post-war pragmatism in our new alliance with Japan saved Hirohito. The Japanese people weren't punished.

Only a decade after the war, the 1956 British film *A Town Like*

Alice was officially withdrawn from the 1956 Cannes Film Festival for fear that it would offend the Japanese. Yet the portrayal of the Japanese was so generous, the Japanese delegation viewing it at a private screening warmly received it.

The long litany of Japanese atrocities during the Second World War hasn't caused revulsion at Asian or Japanese racism the way the Jewish Holocaust caused our obsessive revulsion at white racism. The Japanese were no less convinced of their racial superiority than we were, but the Jewish Holocaust made it untenable for us to impose racial guilt upon other races. I can't think of any films with Imperial Japanese villains, except for the few directly concerning the Asian and Pacific theatre of war. We carefully avoid negative Japanese or other Asian stereotypes, while making them freely about ourselves.

We know the Japanese not by their aggression and cruelty, but their sacrifice and suffering. The most heroic Western soldier laying down his life for God and Country didn't die without needing to die, but the Kamikaze pilots saw glory in suicide.

At the least, we feel pangs of guilt because America dropped atom bombs on Hiroshima and Nagasaki forcing the Japanese surrender. Japan has never felt guilt for anything it did.

At our worst, we condemn our forebears for winning a war we don't condemn Japan for starting or fighting as it did. "*Not forgetting that the largest single-day terrorist attacks in history were committed by this nation & their allies in Hiroshima & Nagasaki,*" wrote Special Broadcasting Service soccer reporter and presenter Scott McIntyre on the 2015 centenary of the Anzac landings at Gallipoli in the Great War, after deriding his compatriots who commemorated his forebears' sacrifice. "*Wonder if the poorly-read, largely white, nationalist drinkers and gamblers pause today to consider the horror that all mankind suffered.*"

Mankind didn't suffer with the bombings of Hiroshima and Nagasaki. Mankind was saved, if only for a while. Fearing more bombs, Japan's quick surrender saved not just American, Australian, and other Western lives. It saved Chinese and other Asian lives too, including the Japanese who'd have died while the war continued.

Germany doesn't become a victim as we've made Japan. We feel no guilt or wreak condemnation about British and American bombers killing something like forty thousand German civilians while destroying the cultural city of Dresden, with little or no military significance, in February 1945.

Rather than becoming frightened of their racism and nationalism, war led Asians to value their races and countries more. The first time I saw a sign in Sydney's Chinatown saying that entry into premises was for "*Asians only*," I was pretty annoyed.

My friend to whom I complained (Ranald from school, for memory, although we were both at university by then) was unconcerned. "Imagine," I said to him, "if there was a club for whites only."

"There is," he replied, "the R.S.L."

The Returned Services League of Australia was a club for soldiers, sailors, and airmen returned from war. When there were too few wars left to fight and past warriors became old, the league changed its name and allowed all former military personnel to join. Without needing to know members, guests from all races can enter club premises to enjoy beer, wine, and meals in congenial atmospheres cheaper than commercial bars and restaurants. No one imagines only white people can come.

My friend's response reflected more than our returned servicemen being white and the country they'd defended being white. It reflected our presumption they were racists: a perfectly acceptable generalisation. The then president of the Victorian Returned Services League Bruce Ruxton wanted Australia to limit Asian immigration, for which we'd widely abused and condemned him.

We don't appreciate their sacrifice. We're too wonderful for that. They were racists.

Asian victims, especially Chinese, periodically complain that official Japanese school textbooks gloss over Japan's wartime record. The only white people complaining were our returned servicemen, but we dismissed our old soldiers' bigotries.

John taught my fourth-form school history class. His son later married a Japanese woman, who showed him a school textbook reducing World War II to a page and a half, calling it a period in which the Emperor received bad advice.

Forty-three years after he taught me, John told the history discussion group he led that public venues in Japan declare themselves open only to Japanese. Their reasoning is that other races would not want to enter them.

While we torment Germans, and Germans torment themselves, for the Holocaust, young Japanese remain ignorant of the slaughters and carnage their race wreaked. They think they'd have won their glorious adventure driving Europeans from Asia but for two American bombs, although the Americans had already taken Iwo Jima. Japan was retreating.

We don't mind. The crimes of Japanese no longer bother us. The crimes of dead Europeans do.

In reviewing the 2003 book *Gold Warriors: America's Secret Recovery of Yamashita's Gold*, Chalmers Johnson suggested there was no point in comparing the relative brutality of Nazi Germany and Imperial Japan upon the peoples they victimised, while noting the punishments meted out upon Germany afterwards as against the relative exoneration offered Japan. Johnson attributed that, in part, to the much greater influence of Jews in America and Britain. *"One reason for these differences is that victims of the Nazis have been politically influential in the US and Britain, forcing their Governments to put pressure on Germany, whereas Japan's victims live in countries that for most of the postwar period were torn by revolution, anticolonial movements and civil wars. This has begun to change with the rise of Sino-American activists."*

I can't help but think that were other races' atrocities through history repeated in documentaries, entertainment, and schoolrooms with the vigour that we talk of our past failings, real and contrived, then we'd hate those races as we hate our past racism. We'd hate Turks, Japanese, and other races for their crimes, most profoundly against us.

With a constant repetition of the pains brought upon people by ideologies, we'd hate ideologies. If all those stupid, awful white racists in films and television shows had been socialists, we'd hate socialists. If we could join mobs hounding down communists, then we'd hate communists for killing Ukrainians with famine. If the people we could so freely hate were Jews, we'd hate Jews.

We hate none of those people. Holding only us accountable, we hate only us.

Atrocities aren't measured by statistics, in a leader board high in the stands. We speak of equating one life with another, one death with another, but the real measures of crimes aren't just the criminals. They're also the victims. The worst of these relative horrors we think are those we commit against others.

10. IMPERIAL CHINA

Chinese communist leader Mao Zedong died in 1976, but is still lying in state in a mausoleum on Tiananmen Square, Beijing. He looked fairly well when I saw him in 1988, for a man who'd been dead twelve years.

Queues to see him separated Chinese, overseas Chinese, and foreigners. Overseas Chinese are the people we call Chinese Americans, Chinese Australians, or even just Americans, Australians, and so forth, but the great-great-grandchildren of émigrés who can't speak any Chinese language and think Ming Dynasty was just the name of a racehorse aren't foreigners in China.

Living in the West doesn't lead us to be loyal to our people and countries. Nor does it diminish other races' loyalties to theirs.

The White House invited Chinese pianist Lang Lang, living in New York, to perform during a state visit by Chinese leader Hu Jintao on the third Wednesday of January 2011. An hour or two beforehand, Chinese everywhere knew what was coming. Enthusiastically they turned to Phoenix Television, China and their computer screens. Lang Lang had chosen to play 'My Motherland', the theme song to the Chinese film *Battle on Shangganling Mountain*. It depicted a group of People's Volunteer Army soldiers hemmed in by the American military until reinforcements arrive and they counter-attack. "When friends are here," says one verse, "there is fine wine, but if the jackal comes, what greets it is the hunting rifle." The jackal is America.

"I thought to play 'My Motherland'," explained Lang, "because I think playing the tune at the White House banquet can help us, as Chinese people, feel extremely proud of ourselves..." He elaborated in writing, "*Playing this song praising China to heads of state from around the world seems to tell them that our China is formidable, that our Chinese people are united; I feel deeply honoured and proud.*"

"In the eyes of all Chinese, this will not be seen as anything other than a big insult to the U.S.," said Yang Jingduan, a Chinese psychiatrist living in Philadelphia and formerly a doctor in the Chinese military. "Lang Lang is expressing the feelings of this generation of angry young people." (The West giving other races so much only makes them angrier for what we've not given them.)

Reading about Lang Lang, I learnt that young Chinese filled computer chat rooms in celebration of the Muslim attacks on America in September 2001 for being an American defeat. I also learnt that the Chinese teach their children that America lost the Korean War. Like most propaganda, it seizes upon a small bit of fact: General Omar Bradley's reference at the time to "the wrong war at the wrong time in the wrong place with the wrong enemy." Chinese call it an admission of defeat, although Bradley had been testifying to the American Congress as to why America should not extend the Korean War into China.

The truth is unimportant. Chinese folklore makes much of a sign allegedly hanging outside a park in Shanghai when European powers controlled parts of China: "*No Dogs and Chinese allowed.*" Many historians believe the sign never existed, but still it featured in the 1972 Hong Kong film *Fists of Fury.*

I learnt of the sign in 2013 after Wang hung a sign outside his Beijing Snacks restaurant near the Forbidden City, Beijing. It read, in its clumsy English translation, "*This shop does not receive the Japanese, the Philippines, the Vietnamese and dog.*"

Filipinos and Vietnamese complained. Chinese didn't.

My Chinese friend Ted was born in Hong Kong where he lived until his parents brought him and his younger siblings to Australia. I met him in our final two years of school, when we no longer played and no longer considered ourselves children, but children we were. Three decades after we finished school together, he was among seven of us old school friends eating dinner at the Great Northern Hotel in Chatswood, including Gregor and our half-Lebanese friend Mark. I'm not sure anyone but I noticed around the walls the black-and-white photographs of old Sydney and colourful prints of oil paintings of old England.

Ted had long ago read several sections from an early draft of what was then a single book I was writing about Western individualism. Since then, I'd divided it into six books, although all he really knew about them were their titles. "Nobody will buy it," he commented of what I then called *New Western Person.* He might have been right, although his reason was the title. "You should call it *New Business Person.*"

Only driving home afterwards, did I understand Ted's suggestion. However passionate he'd been for his Porsche motor car and focused on his financial investments, Ted didn't see himself and other immigrants as Western.

Ted was an Australian citizen, whose daughter learnt Mandarin, Ted once explained, so she could travel. For Ted, a social conscience meant helping other Chinese. He helped start a support group for Chinese consumers and carers in Sydney. He was chairman of the Chinese sub-committee of the Transcultural Mental Health Centre, bringing together dedicated health professionals and community workers for promotional events, education, and Chinese cultural awareness workshops trying to improve mental health among Australian Chinese.

He was Chinese without, it seemed, being any less Australian than I was. Several years earlier, sitting in the Kirribilli Hotel drinking beer, he and his friend Lance knew far more than I knew about the criteria to be chosen Australian of the Year. A champion for multiculturalism in Australia (but not in China), I should have nominated Ted. Demonstrating that immigrants are Australian as we like to do, he was of a right race to win.

"*For more than 20 years,*" complained lawyer Patty Chong in 2008, "*I have championed for a diverse magistracy and judiciary…but all we get are the WASPCs (White Anglo Saxon Protestants/Catholics) and WECs (White European Christians).*" Perceiving people by their race and religion, she presumed her ability had brought her success in her legal career, but only white people's prejudice kept her from achieving more through the thirty-five years she'd been in Australia. She didn't appreciate having been able to come here in the first place and then succeeding as well as she had.

The racial and religious diversity she championed was a selective diversity: only in the West. She can't have liked white people at all.

Neither do we. The first Friday in May 2012, my eldest son and I attended a talk convened by the Sydney–Portsmouth Sister City Committee, commemorating the two hundred and twenty-fifth anniversary of the First Fleet setting forth from Portsmouth in May 1787 to Sydney. The commemoration was a very British event, right down to homosexual Sydney City councillor Phillip Black listing large Chinese populations among the modern-day similarities between the two cities.

The affinity between our two cities was no longer based upon our common race. It was based upon another common race.

In his address, writer Thomas Keneally pointed out that Captain Arthur Philip giving equal rations to convicts and soldiers aboard ship was evidence of our egality, but a woman speaking from the audience instead interpreted Philip's egality as proof that the First Fleet was really an invasion fleet. I was too polite to question Evelyn's leap of self-loathing; she wasn't Aboriginal.

Nor did I say anything when she used my copy of Keneally's recent book, the second volume of *Australians: Eureka to the Diggers*, lying on a table as a rest for writing on her piece of paper. She was quite uppity that I tried to recover my book, expecting me to wait for her to finish using it. I wondered later whether she would've been more polite to me if I were Aboriginal.

Earlier that evening, on the steps outside the beautiful, nineteenth-century Sydney Town Hall, I'd had to persuade one of several Chinese men to permit my son and me to get to our function upstairs. They were only allowing Chinese to enter, attending the grand finale of the Tao Bao Girls 2012 Model Search, Australian Chapter in the hall proper, at which my son and I peeked from an upstairs corridor. The only people in the hall were Chinese, more than a thousand of them, most of whom were rather young. In our Portsmouth gathering, there'd been forty or so Australians, most of whom were rather old.

From a box neglected by a wall, I picked up a Model Search guidebook. It listed the contestants as being Chinese, Indonesian Chinese, Russian Chinese, and so forth. Nationality and country of birth were minor points of distinction. Race was their identity, qualifying them to participate.

In July of 2012, Rachel Chen was crowned Miss Chinese Cosmos Australia in the Melbourne Convention Centre. She would go onto represent Australia at the Miss Chinese Cosmos competition in Hong Kong, competing with Chinese contestants from the Americas, Europe, South East Asia, and China.

In America, the Miss Asian America Beauty Pageant has been running annually since 1985. White Americans are ineligible, without denying Asian women opportunities to be Miss America.

While we lambast our countries and people to the world, other races keep their confidences. While promoting his 2012 film *Chinese*

Zodiac, actor Jackie Chan told Phoenix Television that Chinese should only criticise China in the presence of other Chinese. "If our own countrymen don't support our country, who will?" he asked, oblivious to a West enamoured with most things Chinese. "We talk about" corruption "when the door is closed. To outsiders…, 'our country is the best'."

The citizenship we often trivialise within our countries we expect other countries to respect when our citizens are there. While we describe businesspeople like Stern Hu, James Sun, Matthew Ng, and Charlotte Chou, as well as writer Yang Hengjun, as Australian because of their Australian citizenship, China doesn't. Chinese authorities prosecuted each of them for crimes they allegedly committed in China. "The common feature in all of these cases is that they are ethnic Chinese," said Australian National University legal academic Donald Rothwell in 2011, as if by remarkable insight. The Chinese "really make no distinction" between Chinese citizens and ethnic Chinese with foreign citizenship who return to work in China.

The Australian Department of Foreign Affairs and Trade secretly warned Australian companies not to appoint people racially Chinese to senior executive roles in China. We weren't worried about their loyalties, placing great credence as we do in nationality papers. We wanted to protect them. "It does appear that expatriates of Chinese descent are getting into more trouble," said an Australian consular source in Beijing.

In 2012, Chinese foreign minister Yang Jiechi told Australian foreign minister Bob Carr emphatically that China did "not recognise dual nationality." Chinese people remain, in effect, Chinese nationals in spite of their Western citizenship.

Carr later explained that "the Chinese government does not recognise dual nationality but where Chinese citizens have renounced their Chinese nationality and have entered China on Australian passports, we can gain access to them under our bilateral consular agreement."

China lauds Chinese people bringing capital, technology, and foreign contact to Mother China as *tong bao* (compatriots), whatever their citizenship. Those Chinese are content remaining Chinese, only citing their foreign citizenship when they fall afoul of Chinese authorities and expect those foreign countries to help them. Along with their racial loyalty is their susceptibility to being called foreign agents or spies when things go wrong, said Geremie Barme of the Australian National University.

"Chinese authority is less forgiving of Chinese Australians...," said one anonymous young lawyer. China "still sees them as Chinese first and foremost."

The converse to the Chinese expecting loyalty from fellow Chinese in spite of their foreign citizenship is the loyalty they grant them. The Chinese government intervenes to protect Chinese people overseas, as it did during conflicts with Indonesians in Indonesia in 1965 and '66. The Indonesian-born Chinese were Indonesian citizens whose families had been away from China for generations.

In 1951, while Europeans were withdrawing from our colonies and before we began apologising tirelessly for having been there, China took control of Tibet, formally annexing it in 1959. Gauging public opinion in China at the time is difficult, but there was no audible protest from Chinese people outside China. Chinese colonisation subsequently diluted Tibetan culture, with the most credible estimates of Tibetan casualties in the order of two hundred thousand killed and injured.

In 1989, protesters in Tiananmen Square, Beijing, wanted democratic reforms in communist China. Chinese troops crushed the protests, killing and injuring between two hundred and three thousand Chinese. Chinese people protested the action around the world, as did the West. We protested against the Chinese government, but not China or Chinese people.

In April 2008, the Chinese government's victims weren't Chinese but Tibetans, killed in protests against Chinese rule. Tibetans around the world and many white people condemned the killings. Without talk of equality or diversity, the Chinese government promised to step up the "re-education" of Tibetans to become loyal to China.

Galvanising protests was the Olympic flame ceremoniously lit at Olympia, Greece. Ancient Olympic Games had no flame, but the modern Games introduced them in 1928. Since the 1936 Games in Berlin, the flame has been carried from Olympia through a long list of countries towards the eventual site of each Games. In 2008, as luck would have it, the Games would be in Beijing.

Olympic Games had long stopped having much to do with sport. Zhang Zhuning, chairman of the Chinese Students and

Scholars Association in Canberra, warned that "piles of monks" and Vietnamese thugs from Sydney paid to protest would create trouble for the Olympic flame in Australia. Falun Gong groups were unlikely to cause problems, because Chinese triad gangs had "quietened them down."

Whatever the conflicts between them, Chinese people and their governments stand together in conflicts with others. Defending their country's reputation, thousands of Chinese abused the Tibetan and Western protesters with racial loyalty undivided by nationality. *"Whether you carry a Chinese passport or are an Australian citizen,"* said a letter circulating among Australian Chinese, *"I believe that each and every one of you, the sons and daughters of China, are as one with us in loyalty and love for the motherland!"*

11. BLACK IDENTITY

Journalist Soledad O'Brien, whose father came from Australia and African mother from Cuba, developed and hosted the television series *Black in America*. She and her five siblings had all enjoyed educations from Harvard University, which in 2013 named her a distinguished visiting fellow at the Graduate School of Education. "People would sometimes," she told the Institute of Politics, "when I give speeches, stand up and say, 'You know I think your black America documentaries divisive. I think like, you know, listen, we shouldn't think of ourselves as African American. We're Americans and everybody should stop separating themselves out.'

"First of all it's only white people who ever said that – if we could just see beyond race. If only people didn't see race, it would be such a better place and you are responsible for bringing up these icky race issues Soledad, you should just let sleeping dogs lie. I was like, again, okay white person, this is a conversation you clearly are uncomfortable with and I have no problem seeing race and I think we should talk about race."

White people don't want to talk about race, unless there's something good to say about other races or bad about ours. While other races are inspired by stories of their race doing well, we're most inspired by stories of other races doing well. They included the 2012 Australian film *The Sapphires*, about four Aboriginal women singing for American troops during the Vietnam War. As much as anything else, we interpret their success as being all the greater because we think they're overcoming white racism, instead of being the beneficiary of it.

Not everybody realised. When the film was released on digital versatile disc in America in 2013, the cover was initially tinted sapphire blue, but we care about colour in people more than gemstones. "*The women are Aborigines*," complained white American MaryAnn Johanson on her *Flick Filosopher* website. "*They are black black black black blackety-black black. Not blue.*"

"This is a film about four Aboriginal women who battle against sexism and racism in the 1960s," complained Melbourne climate activist Lucy Manne, who seems not to have been Aboriginal. "Now we've got a D.V.D. cover that is both sexist and racist – it's the antithesis of what the film is about."

Manne's complaint about sexism referred to the cover featuring Irish actor Chris O'Dowd, who played the manager in the film, because he was better known to American audiences than were any of the film's actresses. Even he called the cover "vile." The producers apologised.

Other races talk about race whatever the context. Among the most popular musical figures in America, African American singer Michael Jackson died in 2009. Soon after his death, Bev Smith, host of the *Bev Smith Show* on the American Urban Radio Network, told the *Newshour with Jim Lehrer* that Jackson "belonged to us." Smith's radio show, she said, was aimed at African Americans.

During the scandals threatening Bill Clinton's presidency, African American writer Toni Morrison believed people were too quick to judge him guilty. She called white Clinton "America's first black president," because she felt America was also too quick to judge black people guilty. The phrase was meant to reflect her view about America's treatment of black people as much as anything about Clinton, but it came through the years to imply a special affinity between Clinton and black people.

In 2008, Clinton's wife Hillary, by then a senator from New York, was widely favoured to win the Democratic Party nomination for president. She offered clear, well-researched policies and a senate voting record reflecting middle America. Black America's support for her wavered not so much when Barack Obama announced his candidacy, but when black America realised he could win. Black candidates had contested previous presidential contests, but none were so well organised and resourced. Obama appointed the most talented campaign managers he could, even if they were white.

The only American with whom I spoke about the election at the time remained fearful of Obama. A Benedictine monk, Brother Ned Gerber was troubled not by Obama's race but by him having learnt his politics in Chicago. Ned had lived in Chicago.

In a country where believing in God was still worth more votes than it cost, Obama made much of his twenty years sitting in the church of black clergyman Jeremiah Wright, who blamed the

American government for unleashing the human immunodeficiency virus on black America and accused it of complicity in the 2001 Muslim terrorist attacks on America. Obama never took Wright to task in person, but political expediency in the 2008 campaign demanded he publicly reject both allegations.

Obama delivered a speech titled 'A More Perfect Union' in Philadelphia the third Tuesday of March 2008. "I can no more disown him than I can disown the black community," he said of Wright. "I can no more disown him than I can my white grandmother – a woman who helped raise me, a woman who sacrificed again and again for me, a woman who loves me as much as she loves anything in this world, but a woman who once confessed her fear of black men who passed by her on the street, and who on more than one occasion has uttered racial or ethnic stereotypes that made me cringe."

That capacity to commune with his race and family, with whom he apparently disagreed so much, was probably the most profound thing I heard Obama say. Their commonalities didn't depend on what they believed, but on his common race with Wright and common family with his grandmother. We white people, on the other hand, ostracise each other we consider racist.

"The point I was making was not that my grandmother harbours any racial animosity," Obama elaborated two days later during a radio station interview. "She doesn't, but she is a typical white person, who, if she sees somebody on the street that she doesn't know, well there's a reaction that's in our experiences that won't go away and can sometimes come out in the wrong way."

Racism needn't mean animosity. It can mean generalisation and reaction, based upon experiences.

"And that's just the nature of race in our society," Obama continued. "We have to break through it." He didn't want to break through it too much, when more than ninety percent of black Americans were voting for him in Democratic primaries.

My Jewish friend Ian Biner said that all the Americans he knew were impatient for Obama's victory. At ten thirty-four the last Friday night of November, after his return to Sydney, Ian posted his thoughts under the heading 'Election Fever' on his website. "*I know,*" he wrote. "*The 'Election' is old news, but I was there, in 'Vegas' and watched the whole thing…. I have just one comment…which is that for the few days after Mr Obama won, Americans of a darker colour seemed to hold their chins just a little higher, and their chests just a little further out. Actually, some acted like they own the place. It was nice."*

Canada's Governor General Michaelle Jean called Obama's election part of a "continual story of empowerment," saying it "is a major step not only for the U.S.A., not only for the world's black population, but also for humanity." White Canadians had nominated Jean to be their Queen's representative in Canada, essentially their head of state, although she was born in Haiti and moved to Canada at the age of eleven. It was hard to imagine her being so nominated had she been white.

Presumably that continual story of black empowerment included the Haiti genocide in 1804, when blacks massacred up to five thousand white men, women, and children, including whites who'd been friendly to blacks, to remove white people from the country. The few exceptions to the massacre included whites willing to marry other races.

The empowering of black people that Michaelle Jean described was the disempowering of white people from what had been our countries. She equated advancing black populations with advancing humanity, but nobody says the same of anything advancing white populations. Empowering other races at the expense of our own means humanity overall hasn't benefited, unless we're not part of humanity.

Obama did not break through the nature of race after the election. Nor did he want to.

Standing in the president's office was a bronze statue of Winston Churchill, which the British government had lent to President George W. Bush in 2001 after the Muslim terrorist attacks on America. It reflected Britain and America's historical links, standing together to defeat Nazi Germany in 1945 and against terrorism in the twenty-first century. The British offered to let Obama keep the statue, but he pointedly returned it to the British embassy.

Britain didn't complain, but returning such a gift was a snub unimaginable to other countries. Obama claimed later he thought the office would be cluttered, having brought in a bust of Martin Luther King, but he could've quietly moved Churchill's bust out of his office, along a White House hallway (where another bust of Churchill had been since the 1960s), and even downstairs. He could've stored it in a warehouse on Guam.

The Kenyan's son drew more from a fellow African than a Briton. Racial connections remained, but America was connecting more to Africa than Britain.

Racial democracy is more than just the candidates for whom people vote. It's the other people they prevent from voting.

During the 2008 election, two New Black Panther Party members in black berets, combat boots, shirts, and jackets with military insignias intimidated white voters at a Philadelphia polling place with racial slurs and a nightstick, while a third New Black Panther Party member directed their behaviour. A video camera recorded the incident, which led to a civil complaint against the New Black Panther Party being filed with the Civil Rights Division of the American Department of Justice. It dismissed the complaint.

The American Commission on Civil Rights sought to investigate that dismissal, but the Department of Justice obstructed its efforts. In December 2010, the commission released a report a hundred and forty-four pages long, setting out "*numerous specific examples of open hostility and opposition*" within the department to pursuing cases in which white people were victims.

Christopher Coates, chief of the department's Voting Rights section, testified that some department employees had refused to assist the prosecution of blacks intimidating white Mississippi voters in 2005. Obama's election allowed those most opposed to "race-neutral enforcement" to move into leadership positions at the Civil Rights Division.

They included acting assistant attorney general Loretta King, who'd ordered the dismissal of the New Black Panther case. Christian Adams, lead prosecutor in that case, testified that Department of Justice officials instructed Civil Rights Division attorneys to ignore cases involving black defendants and white victims.

Pursuing those two cases with white victims drew criticism from civil rights groups. They'd not criticised cases Coates brought for black victims there or through his prior work with the American Civil Liberties Union.

At the time of Obama's first inauguration, Maggie and John Anderson of Chicago vowed to patronise only black-owned businesses for a year. It gave rise to what became known as the Buy Black or Empowerment Experiment movement, whose essence was racial loyalty and support among black Americans. Its practical effect was people from other races missing out on trades.

Other races aren't as eager as we are to take backward steps, whenever merit promotes us where they expect to be. While white America still enthused about being led by a black president in 2010, employees at black lifestyle publication *Essence* protested their editor in chief Angela Burt-Murray appointing a white woman, Elliana Placas, to be fashion director. "*It is with a heavy, heavy, heart I have learned that Essence magazine has engaged a white fashion director,*" wrote former fashion editor Michaela Angela Davis. "*This hurts, literally, spiritually. If there were balance in the industry, if we didn't have a history of being ignored and disrespected, if more mainstream fashion media included people of colour before the ONE magazine dedicated to black women 'diversified', it would feel different.*"

Style consultant Najwa Moses agreed. "The fashion industry at large is a very hard place to be if you have a black or a brown face," she said. "*Essence* is the one place we think, 'Oh, if I keep moving up in my career, I might make it there'."

Black American academic Cornel West repeatedly advocated black supremacy in response to white supremacy. He felt Obama didn't do enough for black America.

Speaking to *Ebony* magazine in 2012, black American actor Samuel Jackson was refreshingly candid about matters white Americans aren't. "I voted for Barack because he was black," he said of the 2008 election, "'cuz that's why other folks vote for other people – because they look like them... That's American politics, pure and simple."

For every race but ours, people like them means race. For us, it means wearing a suit.

"When it comes down to it," said Jackson, "they wouldn't have elected a nigger, because, what's a nigger? A nigger is scary. Obama ain't scary at all. Niggers don't have beers at the White House... I hope Obama gets scary in the next four years, 'cuz he ain't gotta worry about getting re-elected."

"Every single thing in my life is built around race," black American actor Jamie Foxx told *Vibe* magazine in 2012, discussing the film *Django Unchained* about slavery, "'cause as black folks we're always sensitive. As a black person, it's always racial."

His racial identity made him proud. "Black people are the most talented people in the world," said Foxx in February 2013, during his acceptance speech at the Image Awards for the National

Association for the Advancement of Colored People. (We dismiss the National Association for the Advancement of White People for its hints of hatred.)

Other races but ours turn to their own for heroes. At the Soul Train Awards in November 2012, Foxx called Obama "Our lord and saviour."

In 2020, American journalists began capitalising *Black* but not *white* when referring to racial groups. The *Columbia Journalism Review* claimed that *Black* is an ethnic designation whereas *white* is merely the skin colour of people tracing *"their ethnic origins back to a handful of European countries."*

The statement was nonsense, but the magazine justified its linguistic genocide *"in light of a global reckoning with race relations"* by discarding *"the largely lilywhite mainstream press"* and *"the style guides that govern their renderings"* to defer *"to writers of colour and to alternative stylebooks."* In other words, writers of colour capitalised *Black*, so we should too.

Black identity, like Asian, South Asian, and American Indigenous identities "include myriad ethnic identities united by shared race and geography and, to some degree, culture," said black journalist Alexandria Neason. She preferred Black to African American and "hyphenated Americanness...which suggests recent ties to the continent."

White people share the same race and geography too, while sharing a wealth of culture, but we respect black identity because black people insist upon their racial identity and ethnic identities, as do Asians, South Asians, and Indigenous Americans. White people have no racial identity or ethnic identities because we do not demand them. We are not allowed to demand them.

Nkweto Nkamba saw the benefit being black can be among white people in the 2014 South Australian local government elections. *"Vote for the black guy,"* said his posters around Parks ward in Enfield, Port Adelaide. "I think it's an education...of what racist is," he said. "People have recognised I'm very comfortable with who I am, people have appreciated that." White people aren't so comfortable with who we are.

12. THE POLITICISATION
OF HISTORY

In communist Warsaw in 1986, Marek told me that schoolteachers taught Polish children that German Nazis massacred the Polish military officers at Katyn during World War II. At home, their Polish parents taught them the truth: Soviet communists murdered the Poles. Since the war, the Soviets had become their allies. The truth had become subversive.

I don't know what proportion of Polish parents corrected their children; totalitarian systems are like that. Only with the end of communism did teachers speak the truth about Katyn.

Early in the new millennium, Western peoples aren't the only races concealing history, and doing it very well. We are the only ones concealing the good in our forebears. We are not the only races manufacturing history, but we are the only ones doing so to malign our forebears.

Families were East Europeans' best defence to Soviet communism, but our families are breaking down under Western individualism. While other races politicise history to promote their race and denigrate others, including us, we politicise history to promote other races and denigrate ours.

The politicised history is often contradictory. Claims of Europe being comfortably multiracial for millennia contradict claims of us oppressing other races for millennia. The only consistent theme is a relentless psychological battle against white people, made worse by the understanding that for us to acknowledge that battle would be racist.

In politicised history, facts do not matter. Ending white people's racism does.

Tom Wills and the other Australians who codified Australian Football in 1859 never alluded to any influence from Aboriginal games. Nobody did, until a hundred and sixty years later. In 2019, the Australian Football League's general manageress of social policy and inclusion, Tanya Hosch, declared that the Aboriginal game Marngrook *"undoubtedly influenced"* Australian Rules football.

That a sporting league even employed a general manageress of social policy and inclusion was telling. What had been Australia's game became an Aboriginal game, without any evidence but Aboriginal elders saying so. Hosch defended the claim from challenge on the basis that Aboriginal and Torres Strait Islander history, perspectives, are always contested or undermined by some people, as if they should never be questioned.

Hosch added that the claim must be true because all eighteen clubs in 2019 signed a statement that it was true: history not by the evidence but by a vote. "This is one of the strongest statements ever made by a sporting code concerning racism in our game and the history of our nation more broadly."

"That just simply is an attempt to rewrite history," said historian Roy Hay. "I have searched high and low, and many other historians have…, to find out if there is substantial evidence that supports that, and really we can find none."

The best the supporters of the claim came up with was that Tom Wills made friends with local Djab Wurrung people during his childhood. Yet the man who felt so warmly towards Aborigines never suggested they had influenced the game. Hay and historian Greg de Moore believed that Wills and his contemporaries borrowed exclusively from the English school games of the time.

Only eleven years earlier, the League commissioned an historian, Gillian Hibbins, to write an essay on Australian football's origins. She said the idea that Australian Rules football originated from Aboriginal games was *"a seductive myth."*

That was only football. Our willingness to lie at the expense of our race betrays no less our forebears who fought.

Sixty-two thousand Australians and eighteen thousand New Zealanders died for the British Empire in World War I. A hundred and fifty-two thousand Australians and forty-one thousand New Zealanders were wounded. A century later, British government briefings on commemorating the centenary of the conflict omitted all mention of them.

They instead spoke of the much smaller numbers of South Asians and West Africans, such as five thousand Nigerians. "It's basically to remind Britons the First World War wasn't just soldiers from here fighting in France and Belgium but involved people from Lagos, Kingston and the Punjab," explained a government insider.

The resulting vision of the war was a lie, trying to create "community cohesion" by linking immigrant races to British history as we've ceased linking any British race to it, justifying more interracial immigration, shaming us out of racial resistance. No longer had the war been fought by the British Empire, or even her successor the British Commonwealth, but what Whitehall called the "new Commonwealth," so visibly not British. Never did our forebears' sacrifice seem more futile, or a British government more neglectful of the people who'd suffered and died for Britain.

When we're not neglecting our histories, we're immersing ourselves in them, wallowing in them, but they're histories of regret. Alone among the races of the world, the themes of Western histories are how horrible we were. Our histories become longer and longer.

Claiming to be up to one-eighth Creek Indian and up to three-sixteenths Cherokee Indian, academic Ward Churchill wrote (alone or with others) fourteen books and more than a hundred and fifty essays accusing white settlers of committing genocide against American Indians and continuing the oppression through his lifetime. In *A Little Matter of Genocide*, he compared white settlement with the Jewish Holocaust and Armenian and Cambodian genocides. In *Kill the Indian, Save the Children*, he described past American and Canadian government policies placing Indian children in residential boarding schools (trying to help them) as genocide.

What made Churchill so fascinating weren't the plagiarism, fabrication, and falsification that ultimately led to the University of Colorado dismissing him in 2007, but that he wasn't part Indian at all. This passionate hater of Europeans was European.

The British Empire had express orders to seek peaceful relations with indigenous races. On the seventh day of September, 1790, twenty or thirty armed Aborigines surrounded a party including the first governor of Australia's First Settlement, Arthur Phillip, at Manly Cove. An Aborigine named Willemering, who we might call a doctor, speared Phillip above his collar bone.

Ordinary military discipline required the perpetrator and his collaborators in the spearing to be executed, but Phillip continued insisting that the British not harm the Aborigines. He said the Aborigine did not realise what he was doing: that it was a cultural misunderstanding.

Like everyone else, Phillip was a white supremacist. White supremacy was a reason not to harm Aborigines but to spare them: to indulge them. It still is.

Being factual isn't enough to make events part of our history that suggest something good in our forebears. Our rewritten history hides the history that no longer suits.

In 1999, David Atfield in Canberra railed against the 1954 British film *The Seekers* for what he construed as its attitudes to European colonisation of New Zealand. "*But what is most distressing about this film,*" he wrote, "*is its assertion that white man and his Christianity saved the Maoris from a savage society constantly at war and brought them peace. In reality white man brought mass slaughter, disease and cultural genocide. I am amazed that as late as the 1950's such imperialist racist attitudes still prevailed.*"

While we cast no blame upon whoever brought epidemics to us, we're not so forgiving of our forebears. Colonial Europeans unwittingly spread disease much as immigrants into the West do now, but accusing immigrants of disease, crimes, and obliterating our cultures would be racist. Suggesting our imperialist forebears did anything else would be racist.

Ten years after Atfield's comments, Peter of New Zealand laughed at his forebears. "*No doubt some humour can be found if, like me, you enjoy marveling at the dated heroic poses often found in these British films made at the fag-end of Empire when Britannia hadn't quite yet waived the rules...*" (His consolation in actors representing their races put further pay to the notion we're blind to race.) "*At least this production has some Maori cast members...*"

In fact, colonial Europeans carried out programmes trying to reduce disease among our dominions. Extensive research by political scientist Robert Woodberry, of the National University of Singapore, established the massively positive influence of Christian missionaries around the world upon education, democratic freedoms, and economic development continuing long after they'd left.

After saying that "such a large population defies stereotyping" in 2009, rugby league coach Roy Masters quoted one Pacific Islander's explanation as to why some get drunk and pass out on the floor, while others are close to their churches and avoid alcohol altogether. The drunkards were Maori from New Zealand where

Christian missionaries had less influence. Tongans, Samoans, and the like enjoyed the benefit of Christian missionaries settling in their islands.

Mere allegations make events parts of our history if they affirm how awful we were. There's no burden of proof for alleging tales of oppression by white people inflicted upon innocent others.

In Western Australia, Aboriginal oral history talks of Europeans massacring Kija Aborigines at Mistake Creek in the 1930s, but there's no police record that such a massacre occurred and no newspapers at the time reported it. That didn't deter Governor General Sir William Deane sixty years later. "I'd like to say to the Kija people," he said, "how profoundly sorry I personally am that such events defaced our land, this beautiful land."

Police recorded a massacre of Aborigines at Mistake Creek in 1915, but with no Europeans involved. It was a massacre of Aborigines by Aborigines.

By the time Deane wrote *Directions: A Vision for Australia*, the problems with the mistaken story of a Mistake Creek massacre didn't deter him from his determination to denigrate his race. *"It matters not whether this particular story is accurate in all its details,"* he wrote, *"for the elements undoubtedly occurred in many parts of our nation in the 211 years of European settlement."*

We're determined to convict us all of past crimes, refusing us doubt, whatever the lack of evidence those crimes occurred. We have only our convictions they occurred and other races concurring.

The events at Mistake Creek, and lack of them, were among several set out in historian Keith Windschuttle's 2002 book *The Fabrication of Aboriginal History*, which ignited an onslaught of verbal assaults from other academics in what were dubbed the history wars. Critics accused Windschuttle of being the equivalent to a Holocaust denier: one of the few Western and many more Muslim historians who either question the occurrence of the Jewish Holocaust during World War II or substantially reduce the estimated number of victims. No insult was greater.

The Holocaust Law, section 130, prohibits Germans from defaming the dead. Germany imprisons people who defame dead Jews by claiming the Holocaust *didn't* occur. We defame our dead by claiming genocides of indigenous peoples *did* occur.

All Windschuttle did was examine the evidence. Pursuing the

truth had become racist, whenever the truth was of our forebears not being as evil as we insist they were. None of the critics diminished Windschuttle's arguments, from what I read, but they remained steadfastly of the view that our European forebears perpetrated widespread and unwarranted mass murder of Aborigines. That's a theme of our history, and we're not willing to lose it.

Six years later, in 2008, Australian parliamentarian Tony Abbott said Australians knowing from where we came was important. *"ok"* responded aka of Sydney on the *News Limited Network* website, without the obvious vitriol other respondents would unleash, *"that's about you Tony but what about other races. they don't have a right to know where they came from?"* Aka was only interested in them.

Abbott believed the primary influences upon us included not just the British Empire but also classical Romans, Greeks, and a little ancient Jewish history. He suggested Australian schools teach history recognising the role played by Britain in shaping the world.

"I agree," responded Simon of Sydney (not me, not with his spelling, grammar, and punctuation), *"lets' teach how the great british empire wrecked the oldest, most stable society in existence. Learn how stupid the entglish were, how many opportunities they squandered. Learn about the great british tradition of swamping communities with dangerous drugs to kill them off. Learn how quickly the british were able to destroy a unique environment and it's people."*

The most intriguing facet of such racial bigotry was that the correspondents condemning the British could well have been British. We describe the white man as if we aren't.

Amidst the abuse we customarily brandish at the British is abuse we brandish at people daring to defend us, as Justin did. After accusing the British of carrying out a *"systematic genocide"* of Tasmanian aborigines, Jeepers of Brisbane went onto tell Justin to *"go back under your rock or you might learn something."*

It's one thing to be ignorant. It's much worse to be certain otherwise.

Examining seventeen volumes of detailed archives, Windschuttle found no evidence of genocide or even of systematic Aboriginal resistance or warfare between Tasmanian Aborigines and the British. There were many instances of conflict through the years, often involving detribalised Aborigines killing settlers, while the British killed a total of only a hundred and eighteen Tasmanian

Aborigines. Most died from disease. The myth of a Tasmanian genocide began with the accusation being made in the 1830s by Henry Melville, editor of the *Colonial Times* newspaper in Hobart, exacting revenge on Governor George Arthur who'd imprisoned him for criminal libel.

Universities might no longer debate matters of race, but they still debate. Windschuttle was among the debaters in a Vice Chancellor's Debate at Macquarie University in August 2008, arguing for the proposition that freedom of speech has its limits. As he explained to me afterwards, that was the argument he was assigned to make. In spite of his stated task, he endorsed writers and speakers controversially challenging popular orthodoxies. Sometimes, deeply offensive ideas eventually replace the orthodoxies they defy, becoming new orthodoxies.

After the formal debate, audience members responded. Speakers other than Windschuttle had criticised the Chinese government's controls on freedom of speech, leading one loyal Chinese person to stand up and passionately defend Beijing. Nevertheless, most people in the primarily white audience voted there should never be controls on freedom of speech (meaning *their* speech).

The debaters and hundreds of audience members then gathered outside in a white canvas marquee. Amidst the glasses of wine, beer, and fruit juice, with slowly appearing trays of small food, Windschuttle was patient, relaxed, and thoughtful, so much so that I wondered if I had his attention. Perhaps our amicable conversation bored him, and perhaps he'd participated in so many they didn't interest him anymore. I wished I could think of something useful to tell him, before he and the other debaters were shortly to slip away and share dinner together, when I mentioned the great enthusiasm of Europeans to find fault in ourselves as other races lack.

"And they don't understand why we do," he remarked, in his casual passing tones.

We lamented people uninterested in learning the facts and even rejecting all notions of fact: relativism. Windschuttle quoted a Canberra university historian saying the only purpose of history is political.

We'd inadvertently digressed to talk about communism, but any discourse about our postmodern West is as much a discourse about communism. The only purpose of everything in our West is political, in this Age of Ideology. Politics prevails, and not just with history. We politicise the past and present into political devices, presuming they already are, with no greater political objective than eradicating white racism. To shame us out of our racism and delegitimise our nationalism, we believe a history of Western oppression and other races' victimhood that is simply untrue.

Among American writer Shannon Kaiser's list of twenty-five habits of happy people in 2013 was making peace with their past. We're at war with ours, consumed with falsehoods about our preceding generations.

My parents' was the last generation that didn't eagerly denigrate times past. The past has become *passé* and we rarely think about it, except being pleased to have left it and deriding anyone unpleased. My generation looks back disparagingly at the era our parents and their parents considered the British the greatest empire the world had known. We see only blood in the maps coloured red, so keen to gloat with our downfall. Never allowing ourselves pride in our people and being Western, being European, our anti-racial arrogance becomes reason to pillory our past.

There's something uncommonly cruel about the way we malign our forebears who wanted the best for us, damning our builders of empire for the racism we respect in other races. It's a massive injustice against them and us, manipulating us in our dealings with other races and in our sense of ourselves. We don't pursue knowledge about them and their circumstances that don't fit our vision of history, knowing they were racists. Our prejudices against them deny us scope to assess their thoughts and deeds fairly. We don't want to be like them.

More than our shame is our pride as we assail our shameless forebears. We make ourselves better than those ignorant wrongdoers, we solitary pinnacles of how wonderful we are, without being so racist as to think we're better than other races.

13. WHITE RACIAL GUILT

Among the scientists performing experiments upon gypsies at the Auschwitz-Birkenau concentration camp during World War II was paediatrician Berthold Epstein, to whom Norway had granted asylum before her German invasion. Following orders under threat of death was normally no defence from prosecution at the Nuremberg trials after the war (when we were suddenly expected to have been rebellious individuals willing to die to save Jews), except that Epstein was a Czechoslovakian Jew. His family died in Auschwitz.

We forgave him. We allow other people's racial links to excuse them from crimes for which they would otherwise be guilty. We impose our racial links to punish ourselves for crimes of which we're otherwise innocent.

Amidst our individualism, we rarely apologise to each other anymore. Amidst our rejection of racism, we now apologise to everyone else. In our endless pursuit of apology, the only apologies more commonplace than ours for what we think are our present-day failings are ours for what we think were our forebears' past failings.

In 2002, Prime Minister Helen Clark offered "a formal apology to the people of Samoa for the injustices arising from New Zealand's administration of Samoa in its earlier years, and to express sorrow and regret for those injustices." She was particularly "troubled by some unfinished business," meaning the steamship S.S. *Talune*, which inadvertently brought a worldwide influenza epidemic from New Zealand to Apia in 1918. The pandemic gave rise to the Samoan independence movement. New Zealand police armed with rifles and a machine gun killed at least nine Mau protesters in 1929. Samoa was known as Western Samoa until 1997.

Eighty years onward and forty years after their independence, the depth of New Zealand's apology surprised the Samoans. They'd not asked for one.

We don't just deem our forebears to have been wrong. We make them representative of us. They and the peoples we say they mistreated are often long dead, but theirs was no individual guilt. It's our racial guilt. We recognise our race every time we feel ashamed for what our people did, or we're told our people did. Our histories are racial: racial crimes transcending successive generations. We're painfully aware that we're white.

The last Thursday in May 2008 was my eldest son's first experience of Reconciliation Day at high school. The particular day that schools nominate seems to vary, but it's always in Reconciliation Week. The reconciliation to which they refer is a particular reconciliation: that between Aborigines and white Australians. It's predicated upon race. Any relationship between races has to be racial.

Not satisfied with apologising every year anyway, the Australian government officially designated 2008 the Year of the Apology. The posters around my eldest son's high school made it clear whose apology it was, by one race to another. Instead of being denied the chance to identify with our race, we're compelled to identify with it whenever time comes to apologise. The multitude of other races at the school could walk by unconcerned.

Instead of our children seeing images of great Western scientists, composers, and artists, reconciling themselves with themselves, the morning assembly for years seven to ten comprised a presentation of notable Aborigines: authors, activists, politicians, and sportspeople, whose photographs were projected onto screens at the front of the hall. Speakers recited their achievements, while Aboriginal music played in the background.

Enjoying nothing more than making a good apology, we trawl through history books looking for other people's suffering so we can flagellate ourselves. "*Along came Robert Clive and the East India company*," complained Robert Rowan of Adelaide in response to Tony Abbott wanting Australians to learn of the British Empire, "*out with their bibles and down at the docks...loading the goodies as fast as they could!*"

In fact, British rule over India followed the much longer-lasting Mongol Mughal Empire, unknown to us today. Internecine violence was so severe and widespread during the nineteenth century that the Indian population was falling until the East India Company and then the British Crown and Empire brought order.

An Indian-born teacher of English as an Additional Language or Dialect at our youngest children's high school credited the British Empire with developing Indian nationalism. Warring tribes and warlords gave way to nationalism when the British built railroads connecting them, she told me in November 2017. With nationalism, came peace.

The racism we condemn isn't just prejudice. It's feeling at all good about us.

In 2012, students of St Paul's College, Sydney University convened a dinner with the theme: the end of the British Raj. Dressed in colourful traditional garments, Indian and other South Asian waiters served Indian curries and delicacies to the college students dressed in formal attire.

"I do not think the party was a celebration of Indian culture," complained arts student Mason McCann. (Such a celebration would've been fine.) "It was a celebration of imperialism.... I am deeply offended by it." The positive images we should present are of Indian culture and history, not ours. "They have a responsibility as a prestigious and old institution to project a positive public image to both the other students and the public, and I think that party succeeded in doing just the opposite of that."

The *Honi Soit* student magazine published McCann's letter of protest igniting the controversy in full. It edited the response of St Paul's resident Hugo Rourke.

South Asians quickly chimed in, claiming to have suffered under British colonialism. "Most of the people who said it wasn't racist were white people who go to college or have friends in college, but the non-whites were quite upset about it," said Student Representative Council welfare officer Rafi Alam, a Bangladeshi. He said the party proved a "racial subtext" existed at Sydney University. Ours is a racial culpability, not just in our sad, sorry eyes but in the angry eyes we inflame in the rest of the world.

Immigration prevents us celebrating our people's past, as it's supposed to do, but Ram Devagiri, the state manager of catering company Sodexo, said the South Asian waiters worked at St Paul's College every day. "They are not happy that they are being dragged through this, because they actually had a great time that evening."

In terms of the law, the New South Wales Anti-Discrimination Board president Stepan Kerkyasharian said there'd been no unlawful discrimination, because there'd been no insistence that only people from the Indian subcontinent serve as waiters. Re-enacting the British Raj "may offend some people but I don't think the act itself constitutes discrimination or vilification... I think if" an historical re-enactment "is done accurately and in good faith and the re-enactment itself is not offensive, is not intended to vilify and is not discriminatory, then one has to accept the historical reality. If the message here was, 'Look, Indians are slaves...or Indians are only good as waiters' I would find that objectionable, but if the intent was to create this historical imagery...I wouldn't see that as deliberately derogatory or deliberate vilification of people of an Indian background."

Any celebration of our history is "fraught with danger," said Stephen Gapps, curator at the Australian National Maritime Museum. "I think some events are difficult to re-enact because of the long memories of the terrible events, particularly colonial stuff and the U.S. Civil War. Some things should not be re-enacted, like events from the Holocaust." Portraying the history that remains requires sensitivity to "get people from both arguments involved in the beginning." The result is something cathartic rather than divisive, but never anything of which we can be proud.

The secretary of the Australasian Living History Federation, Jessica Robinson, said re-enactments done sensitively don't glorify slavery, Nazism, religious hatred, or the conquest of Aborigines. "Our main rule is that we don't want re-enactment to be a vehicle for any kind of political ideology that someone is trying to force through in the modern era."

Well, some ideology anyway. Denigrating Europeans is fine. Applauding us isn't. Applauding other races is fine. Denigrating them isn't. Through May and June 2013, the Australian National Maritime Museum celebrated everything Indian.

Convulsed with the sense we're the worst of all races, our principal postmodern shame remains the mandatory migration of Africans, centuries ago. Slavery still soiled mayor Ken Livingstone's London in 2007.

Livingstone didn't apologise for much in his life, but he apologised for events long before he was born, to people who'd known only modern Britain's largesse. "You can look across there to see the institutions that still have the benefit of the wealth they created from slavery," he claimed, speaking of his forebears in the third person as if they were another race altogether. He refused to attribute London's financial strength to anything good about them.

His response was emotive, not factual, as our thoughts about race have increasingly become since the Holocaust. While individual traders and plantation owners profited from slavery, poor Europeans lost for being denied jobs. The overall monetary role played by slavery was much less than the sugar sweetening rich people's tea. Bringing home tobacco from the Americas proved harmful. The Industrial Revolution was central to our growing wealth, but slaves lacked the skills, dexterity, and temperament for factories. They worked on farms where the labour was menial. The British Empire would continue improving for another eighty years after emancipating all slaves in 1834. The biggest problem was wondering what to do with the freed.

Slavery has been commonplace around the world throughout history. Europeans didn't invent slavery, although the modern word "slavery" comes from the same Greek word as "Slav" after Vikings captured and enslaved so many Central and East Europeans. Viking invaders of northern England took Saxon homes and enslaved my ancestors, too.

Black American writer Toni Morrison said much about the slavery of Africans in her 1987 novel *Beloved*. Her lesser-known 2008 novel *A Mercy* explored slavery not premised upon race. The latter described the seventeenth-century experiences of a black slave, an American Indian servant, and two white indentured servants after the white farmer to whom they were charged died of smallpox.

Most indentured servants and slaves in Britain's colonies through the seventeenth century were Irish, including political prisoners, petty criminals, and people simply kidnapped from Ireland. During the 1650s, Britain took a hundred thousand Irish children aged from ten to fourteen years old from their parents and sold them as slaves in Virginia, New England, and the West Indies.

The distinction between slavery and indentured service could be technical. Slaves were the subject of property rights traded with others. Indentured servants were bound by contractual rights, but indentured labour became like slavery while debts were unpaid and the labourers were traded like slaves. Both were premised upon class and sometimes, but not always, upon race. British traders enslaved poor Britons and others to work in her colonies, including tens of thousands of children. Indentured labour was often entered into voluntarily, but poor Europeans had few other options. Many were consigned to the Americas.

What mattered most to the people concerned was how horribly or well they were treated. Many cheap Irish were treated worse than more expensive Africans were treated.

As well as African slaves, Britain transported involuntarily to America an estimated fifty thousand convicts, almost all of whom were British or Irish. After American independence, Britain transported a further hundred and sixty-five thousand convicts to Australia, the last of whom arrived in 1868. All but a thousand or so of them were European.

They too had little choice in their journeys, but we don't worry about them. Our emancipation of other races no longer extends to our own.

We blame ourselves for having participated in slavery without giving ourselves credit for ending it. In 1839, Englishman Joseph Sturge founded the world's oldest human rights organisation, Anti-Slavery International, to campaign to outlaw slavery everywhere. Personifying the benevolent British Empire long after she'd abolished slavery, David Livingstone (no relation to Ken) set about ending slavery by Arab and Portuguese slave traders he came across in Africa. In many cases, the initial enslavement of Africans wasn't by European conquest but by fellow Africans wanting to trade.

Lieutenant General Robert Baden-Powell led the British expeditionary forces during the Anglo-Ashanti wars. In his 1896 diary, he recorded *"the main reasons and objects for the expedition: – To put an end to human sacrifice. To put a stop to slave trading and raiding. To ensure peace and security for the neighbouring tribes…"*

Baden-Powell added: *"…in no part of the world does slavery appear to be more detestable than in Ashanti…They are wanted for human sacrifice. Stop human sacrifice, and you deal a fatal blow to the slave trade, which you render raiding an unprofitable game."*

In 1901, parliamentarian Thomas Bayley noted in the House of Commons that *"…in 1896 the King of Ashanti was the most cruel and heartless man this world ever produced."* Britain reviewed its role in the conflict, concluding that errors might have been made in offending King Prempeh I and his supporters but ending slavery was a moral imperative.

In 1923, the Parliamentary Under Secretary of State for the

Colonies, William Ormsby-Gore, reiterated our concern for Africans. "The Secretary of State sees no reason to doubt that Prempeh's deportation was necessary in the interests of Ashanti," he said.

Slavery didn't inspire the American Civil War as much as the anti-slavery abolitionists threatening to intervene in the slave states without fair compensation for abolishing slavery or sensitivity to the implications of doing so. (We're so pleased they did.) President Abraham Lincoln's opposition to slavery was pivotal to the war. With the conflict already won, he prolonged the killing to pass the Thirteenth Amendment to the Constitution, if the 2012 film *Lincoln* is anything to go by.

We're relaxed about the deadliest war in American history, when we construe it as a war to liberate Africans. When brother fought against brother, we made family less important than causes, statehood, and nationalities.

Since then, the West has lost the statehood and nationalities, but still has ideas to be our causes. White Americans fought more with each other than black America over racial integration through the 1960s. White Americans fight with each other on other races' behalf.

Our culpability for slavery flashed to mind in 2011 when I saw the newspaper headline, 'British woman convicted of slavery.' The slave was a Tanzanian, Mwanamisi Mruke. "From the moment of her arrival in England," prosecutor Caroline Haughey told Southwark Crown Court, "Mwanamisi was made to sleep, work, and live in conditions that fall, by any understanding, into that of slavery." Her mistress was a former hospital director who'd brought Mruke from a hospital she owned in Dar es Salaam. The mistress we called British was Saeeda Khan.

In the 1960s, Indian communists Aravindan and Chanda Balakrishnan immigrated to Britain. They kept three women slaves (a Briton, an Irishwoman, and a Malaysian, presumably celebrating diversity) in a London house for thirty years until 2013.

Slavery doesn't require trade. Nor does it require Europeans. In 2013, one in five people in Mali were slaves.

While the African slave trade to the Americas was getting under way, Italian merchants were transporting Bulgarian and other slaves to satisfy North African traders. Muslim Istanbul imported as many as two and a half million European slaves from 1450 until 1700.

Tucked away at the peripheries of literature are books like Giles Milton's *White Gold*, which tells of a fleet of Muslim corsairs early in the eighteenth century attacking a Cornish fishing village, carrying an eleven-year-old lad and other villagers to the Moroccan port of Salé to be sold as slaves. From the sixteenth century, North Africans snatched more than a million white European slaves in raids on coastal towns in England, Italy, France, Spain, Portugal, the Netherlands, and Iceland to be traded in markets along the Barbary Coast of North Africa, including what is now Morocco, Algeria, Tunisia, and western Libya. Conquest by France ended the white slave trade in 1830.

Ours is a selective individualism. Identifying with victims because we're of the same race would be racist. Identifying with wrongdoers of our race we do freely.

While we erupt in a frenzy at the wrongs our people committed against others, we're uninterested in their crimes against us. Other races shine in our eyes so much as to blind us, while our race burns in our brains. Rather than imagine we have no greater guilt than those North Africans and other Africans, Arabs, and Turks, we allow the guilt for slavery to be ours alone. We escape white people's past racism with white people's proud guilt.

Our forebears' legacy is all that remains for them to suffer: their punishment for our racial guilt. We're races convicted of past wrongfulness. Cruel corruption of history it might be, but we damn white descendants of slaves for the crime of slavery, while honouring as victims the African and Arab descendants of slave traders and keepers.

14. OTHER RACES' INNOCENCE

Building empires was never unique to Europeans. Other races fought, conquered, and ruled each other, killing and pillaging. Aztecs, Mayans, and Incas carved their empires across their fellow Native Americans, Pacific Islanders cut theirs across each other.

From 1206, Genghis Khan led the Mongol hordes, conquering much of Asia. Without thought of bettering the lives of local people, Mongol invasions committed atrocities on unarmed populations, spreading fear.

In 1223, the Mongol Empire reached Eastern Europe, conquering Volga Bulgaria and Kievan Rus'. Mongols laid siege to Moscow in 1238 and slaughtered the inhabitants of Kiev in 1240. From 1237 to 1240, Mongols destroyed most of the major cities of Russia.

The Mongols invaded Poland in 1240, destroying the city of Lublin. They invaded Hungary in 1241, killing half the population. They invaded the German principality of Margravate of Meissen, burning most of the city of Meissen. They attacked Austria, murdering the largely unarmed residents of Wiener Neustadt, south of Vienna before the Austrians drove them out. Mongols also attacked Bohemia, where the kingdom's defences discouraged them and Bohemian forces warded them off.

Mongols invaded Serbia and Bulgaria in 1242. Legend has it they attacked Croatia in the battle of Grobnik field. Mongols attacked the Latin Empire of Constantinople.

The Mongols continued raiding Europe late into the thirteenth century. They again invaded Poland in 1259 and 1287. They again invaded Hungary in 1285.

Early in February 2001, during time between meetings on my second business trip to Perth, I visited an exhibition on Genghis Khan and the secret history of the Mongols. (Few things were more natural about my business trips than taking every chance I could to explore.) What struck me, and I think struck the law firm lawyer with me after I mentioned it to him, was the pride Mongols held for the man we equated with bloodshed and terror.

The themes of Asian countries' histories are how great, civilised, or pure they are. We agree. We don't condemn other people's empires as we condemn our own, associating Khan with less bloodshed than we associate ourselves. We don't find Asian imperialism offensive as we find past European imperialism. They are the glorious others.

We look upon the failings of people from other races in a very different light to the failings of people from ours. On Maundy Thursday 2015, after lining up students who weren't Muslim at the Garissa University College in Kenya, Al Shabaab gunmen massacred a hundred and forty-eight of them, primarily Christians. In response to a note of the massacre on the Facebook compute site, white Australian Caroline Pidcock thought no less of Muslims or Africans. She thought less of everyone. *"Terrible,"* she wrote on Easter Day. *"Who have we become?"*

As much as a statement of our shared culpability, hers was a statement of our loss of identity. I daresay the Al Shabaab gunmen had clear senses not just of their identities but of Pidcock's white Christian identity, as she did not.

The phrase "Man's inhumanity to man" (no problem with sexism there) is the means by which the West takes responsibility for the wrongdoings of other races. The phrase isn't applied to Western wrongdoings; man's inhumanity to man fades from earshot. Other people's failings are the failings of all of us. Our failings are ours alone.

When we look beyond wider responsibility to hold people of another race guilty of a crime, their guilt is individual. Cambodians revile communist dictator Pol Pot (a former Buddhist monk) and his henchmen for the murder of up to a million seven hundred thousand people from 1975 until '79. We revile him too, but only him; we don't know those henchmen's names. We don't blemish all Cambodians for the crime; theirs isn't a Cambodian or communist shame. Nothing taints other races like that staining Europeans. We don't make their governments and companies representative of their innocent races.

If the Cambodian Genocide isn't a human shame, then we're to blame. Australian journalist John Pilger, who'd initially supported Cambodian communists as he supported communists everywhere, blamed Americans for the Cambodian Genocide by blaming them for Pol Pot coming to power, against the backdrop of the neighbouring Vietnam War. He didn't blame Vietnamese or Cambodians.

We hold each other, or ourselves, accountable for other people's bad deeds and ills when there's any means to do so. We can find vicarious racial guilt for any crime on earth.

European empires kept African tribes from killing each other, but the conflicts we controlled through our era of empire resumed when we departed. During the hundred days of the Rwandan Genocide in 1994, Hutus massacred at least eight hundred thousand Tutsis and thousands of moderate Hutus, but we don't let them besmirch Africans in general or Hutus in particular. Not merely humanity's shame, we managed to cast specific blame on the West for not having intervened in that internal affair of a sovereign African country. I can't imagine what we could have done, short of returning to empire.

Paradoxically, we also blamed the genocide on Belgium once controlling the country. (We find a way to blame most problems of the world upon European colonialism.) Thirty-two years after her departure wasn't enough to make the Hutus accountable for their actions.

In the 2004 film *Hotel Rwanda*, a character claims Belgian colonists invented the distinction between Hutus and Tutsis. In fact, it already existed.

My Chinese accountant friend Peter hired a banquet room at a Chinese restaurant for his buck's night dinner in 1995, when peace in Europe appeared eternal and French nuclear weapons tests seemed unnecessary. Sometime before the strippers came, conversation turned to the French government testing nuclear weapons on the uninhabited Mururoa atoll in French Polynesia. Opinion around the table derided not just the French government but all the damned French, when I pointed out, "The Chinese are also testing nuclear weapons."

China had the world's fourth largest nuclear weapons arsenal, but didn't suffer the criticism so freely levelled at France. The white Australian waiter interrupted tending to his customers to defend China. "They're doing their testing in their backyard," he told me, referring to Xinjian, home to the minority Uighurs.

"France regards its overseas territories as France," I said, but none of it mattered to the Asians or Australians around me. They lambasted the French for doing what they excused, even endorsed, the Chinese doing.

Our shared sense of being Western helps us dislike each other: another paradox regarding our treatment of race. We return to race to berate each other and excuse other races, judging Europe and the West as we don't judge anyone else. The younger of my sisters, as vitriolic as anyone in criticising French nuclear testing, explained the difference not by condemning her fellow Europeans but by embracing them. "We're civilised," she told me.

Ours are the high standards we must uphold, whatever other races do. We fail to warrant excuse, too arrogant for that.

Late in 2011, I was in Melbourne for a mining and energy lawyers' conference. Near the conference venue was the Old Treasury Building, where some exhibitions took advantage of a strange quirk from history. In the nineteenth century, the poor people most likely to be photographed were criminals because gaols used the new technology to identify incoming prisoners. Several photographs were displayed with stories accompanying them.

Between the gold vaults downstairs, the *Forgotten Faces* exhibition focused upon *"Chinese and the Law."* A country founded as a penal colony offered many exhibitions mentioning people committing crimes in the colonies and in Britain from which we came, but this was the first I saw to point out that not every person was a criminal. As an exhibition board expressed it, *"A very small proportion of the Chinese immigrants committed crimes and were imprisoned."*

They weren't just a small proportion but a *very* small proportion. It was the same for the British and Irish, but we never bothered to mention it. The exhibitions upstairs in the Old Treasury Building hadn't mentioned it, not even the one focused upon women prisoners. They were all, or nearly all, European.

Not content with such disclaimer was the next board, headed *"Chinese and the Law in the Colony of Victoria."* It would be easy to forget that the exhibition was about Chinese criminals, including those convicted of murder, because only Europeans were described with disdain, and quite a bit of it, in an exhibition not even about us. *"From the time of their arrival in Victoria in the 1850s the Chinese met with racism and ignorance. Their presence in large numbers on the goldfields provoked a great deal of resentment and unrest as a result of xenophobic and economic anxieties."*

A year earlier, at the Bathurst Goldfields museum, my elder children and I had seen the same obsession with instances of our hostility to Chinese labourers during the nineteenth-century gold rushes supposedly only because Chinese were hard working. They were postmodern interpretations of events a century and a half earlier, expressing our historical theme of our supposed victimisation of others.

Between visiting those two places, in April 2011, my elder three children and I took a walking tour through the small town of Hill End. The tour guide, whose family had lived in Hill End through four generations, taught us a history we'd never before heard, although Sandra spoke without judgement of the Chinese as we spoke in judgement of our forebears.

Firstly, she told us that Chinese entrepreneurs had brought the Chinese labourers to Australia in the first place. Only after working long enough hours and finding enough gold to pay set amounts to their Chinese bosses, could they return home. The people exploiting the Chinese were Chinese.

Secondly, many Chinese men married white Australian women and had children. When they could return home to China, they did, without thought of taking their white wives or mixed-race children with them. China remained Chinese, the rest of the world for mixed-race offspring.

Thirdly, Sandra spoke of the early years in the twentieth century, when Hill End was long past her glory days. All most of us knew of the time was the White Australia Policy, with our usual presumptions of white cruelty to other races. In Hill End, an old Chinaman who'd remained after the gold rushes suffered arthritis. In spite of their own hard times, white people bought produce from him purely to give him money with which to live. Sandra was proud of the help our people gave him, as she seemed prouder of nothing else we'd done. They were stories the like of which I've not heard again.

European colonial powers built empires with thought of helping not just themselves but also local populations, even if events sometimes panned out otherwise. The most aggressive were the Spaniards and Portuguese who'd suffered centuries of occupation at home by North African Moors. The shipping superintendent for TNT Shipping & Development Limited and then Holyman Limited later worked in Uruguay, which he noticed suffered none of the issues with indigenous peoples that other countries did. He mentioned it to a Uruguayan, who replied matter-of-factly, "We killed them all."

If other arms of the Spanish Empire or other European Empires had wanted to carry out genocide of Indigenous tribes and races, then we would have carried it out. Indigenous tribes and races survived because we didn't want to kill them, beyond what conquest and defence required. Our Empires secured, we tried to help them.

We're relaxed about the benefits to other European countries of Roman and Napoleonic invasions, but refuse to see benefits to the world from Europe's age of global empire. Suggesting local people derived any benefit from European colonisation has become taboo, but standing in Melbourne is a monument to Major-General Charles Gordon of the Royal Engineers. The Chinese emperor had already honoured him for being among the European officers leading Chinese soldiers in the Ever Victorious Army, which helped end the Chinese civil war known as the Taiping Rebellion in 1864. *"He rescued provinces from anarchy, but would accept no reward."* As governor-general of the Sudan, he did much to end slave trading, before being beheaded at Khartoum in 1885.

When we're not encouraging other races to hate us, they don't think our empires were bad. On the second Thursday of March 2013, the *South China Morning Post* website began a poll asking the people of Hong Kong: *"Would Hongkongers vote to return to a British overseas territory, given the option?"* A week later, ninety percent of respondents had answered, *"Yes."*

Dare I feel pride for our past? We stood tall among races and built wonderfully impressive empires, making mistakes but sharing civilisation with the world: arts, culture, government, and society. We fostered science, technology, and innovation, the like of which no other races have.

Dare I call myself proud of the greatest empire the world has ever witnessed? Without it, I wouldn't exist.

Being born is a miracle, from an instant of space and time. Another moment and each of us wouldn't exist. Oh, another person might've existed, but that person wouldn't be each of us. If our mothers never met our fathers, we would never have been born. For us colonial children, that our mothers could have met our fathers becomes inconceivable if our empires hadn't brought them together. It's the same realisation children of immigrants cite to defend their parents coming, without which they mightn't exist.

More than anyone dead, I'm saddened for the people still alive. We've lost the joy of having come into existence. The sons and daughters of empire who despise the empire from which our forebears were born despise having been born. Our rejection of our empires and colonialism is colonial Europe's despair at being alive.

Saint Barbara is the patron (although that should be matron) saint of miners. For her, as well as for the beer, wine, and company, several aged geologists, engineers, and supporting professionals gather for lunch somewhere in northern Sydney the first Friday each December. When I first attended St Barbara's Day lunches, from 2001 at the Malaya restaurant in North Sydney, close to fifty of us were there: a rare group of white Anglo-Saxons, almost all of us men. By 2008 at the Spicy Wok restaurant in Crows Nest, only ten of us attended. I, then forty-six years of age, was the youngest.

Sitting aboard a train that afternoon, headed back to work, four loud and raucous young men strode into the carriage, slapping their hands and laughing. They slumped into a pair of three-people seats facing each other. They spoke without accents, so the West insists they were simply Australians, but I'd been writing about our postmodern West too long to ignore reality. They were two East Asians and two Middle Easterners.

In spite of the laws and signs that passengers not put their feet onto seats, an East Asian did. Perhaps the others did too; I couldn't see their knees from where I sat as I saw his knee bent high. Laws and signs prohibited smoking, but the other East Asian pulled out a plastic pouch of tobacco, small round white filter, and rectangle of white paper. He rolled himself a cigarette. We treat our countries with such contempt, we can hardly expect better from other races.

The West would cast my experience aside because they're sure they've seen white Australians do the same, but I'd not seen feet on seats for many years and I'd never before seen anyone prepare a cigarette aboard a Sydney train. They'd insist we tolerate their behaviour, and add that we should've helped them and their parents understand our laws and customs, as if they cared.

In all events, what struck me most about them was their self-confidence, even arrogance, as our young people lack. (What we disparagingly call arrogance in white people we affectionately call self-confidence in others.) They were much like the tall East Asian in the Art House Hotel bar the previous evening, whose head held high, hair swept brashly back, and confident demeanour can only have helped him dominate the group of young white men and women congregating with him.

White people can be self-confident, but only for our wealth, jobs, or politics. We're nothing without them. It's arrogance reserved in spite of our race, denied to those of us without money, careers, and ideology. I've never seen a self-confident poor white person, but I've seen a lot of self-confident poor among other races. We lambast the arrogant rich among our race, but never arrogance in the rich of other races.

For that, I envied those four aboard the train. They weren't growing up being told the world was unjust for what their awful race had done, as young white people are. They were growing up assured the land was theirs along with their ancestral lands, proud of what their people did.

If we're not yet willing to feel pride in our people and past, we can at least accord them fair value. We can see the good as much as the bad in our forebears and in other people's forebears, presuming neither goodness nor badness of anyone. Denying our children the chance to love themselves is the cruellest and most horrific abuse.

15. WHITE PEOPLE'S HEROES AND HEROINES

On the last Sunday in May 2012, I stood in the prestigious Abbotsleigh private girls' school. I had to smile, for among the posters the rich schoolgirls had drawn objecting to oil exploration and people wearing animal furs was another expression of our postmodern obsession with equality. A little incongruous in an Anglican Church school steeped in wealth and privilege, the equality the girls wanted wasn't between rich and poor white people. Their poster referred to black American clergyman Martin Luther King and white American writer Harper Lee, a Methodist.

So far as we knew at the time, Lee only wrote one novel, *To Kill a Mockingbird*, first published fifteen years after World War II. Her poetic introduction captured much of lost childhoods and old Alabama, which the 1962 film captured less well. It focused on the theme that made the book significant. Horrible white people falsely accused a black man of raping a white girl, but the heroic white lawyer Atticus Finch proved his innocence to the reader and viewer as he couldn't to the racist white jury.

At the time, most Americans would've said racism was natural and acceptable, but after the horrors of the Holocaust in Europe, they were ready to disagree. More importantly, the minority of people condemning racism had voices: loud voices. They gave Lee's book the 1961 Pulitzer Prize and a place on school syllabuses. It went onto become the most widely prescribed book for school reading lists across Britain, North America, and Australasia. For many white children, it was their introduction to black men.

Almost half a century after publication, the book headed a poll conducted for World Book Day in 2006 by the Museum, Libraries, and Archives Council. Better versed in books than in grammar, the council asked British librarians, "Which book should every adult read before they die?" The Bible came second.

In 2007, America's President George W. Bush awarded Lee the Presidential Medal of Freedom. In 2011, English footballer David

Beckham and his singer wife Victoria named their fourth child Harper in her continuing honour, although Victoria had famously remarked that she'd never read a book. She might've read *To Kill a Mockingbird* since making that remark, but we don't need to have read it to know its great theme.

The book so dear to us for revealing what we think to be true was a work of fiction. Lee loosely modelled Atticus Finch on her father Amasa Coleman Lee, at various times a lawyer, newspaper proprietor, and Alabama state legislator who'd supported strict racial segregation before becoming caught up in the black civil rights movement of the late 1950s.

In 1919, he'd defended two black men charged with murder. If racial prejudice underpinned public attitudes towards the accused, then it was well placed. There's no evidence the men were anything but guilty of the murder with which they were charged, convicted, and hung, but Lee never handled a criminal case again. If he suffered guilt for his inability to save the men from the noose, then he might've imagined them being innocent. His daughter's imagination passed the blame to other white Alabamans, making her father the hero. Devoted daughters imagine all sorts of features in their fathers.

Being fictitious doesn't bother us. No other races make so central to their literature a story of their race mistreating another, but books are about heroes. The hero of *To Kill a Mockingbird* was from our race: Atticus Finch. At a time in our histories we're groping for something good in us in which to believe, there's no more heroic an act for a white person than to fight other white people's prejudice.

Without racial identities, we've lost commonality with our great writers, artists, and composers. Instead, our commonality is with anyone who opposed our racism. We still have Harper Lee, but also Herman Wouk.

An American Jew, Wouk won the Pulitzer Prize for Fiction in 1952 for *The Caine Mutiny*, which became the major novel I studied in my last year of school. Most memorable of that most memorable book was Jewish lawyer Barney Greenwald declaring that without American naval officers like the tyrannical Captain Queeg, Greenwald's mother could have been "*melted down into a bar of soap.*"

Our heroes fight white racism as did Atticus Finch and, incidentally, Captain Queeg. Forty-four years after the Mexico City

Olympic Games in 1968, Australian human rights lawyer Jennifer Robinson called Australian athlete Peter Norman her Australian Olympic hero, but not for winning a silver medal in the two hundred metres sprint. While black American medal winners Tommie Smith and John Carlos raised their clenched fists in black gloves in their black power protest from the victory dais, Norman supported them by wearing an Olympic Project for Human Rights badge.

Other races make heroes and heroines of people from races not theirs when those people help their race, not when they work against it. Justice Marcus Einfeld's conviction for perjury didn't diminish my Chinese friend Ted's respect for the Jew who'd promoted Australia accepting more Asian refugees and other immigrants. Making false statutory declarations were among many lies Einfeld was found to have made, although his other lies weren't criminal offences.

Nor could anything Al Grassby do diminish Ted's affection for the half-Spaniard, half-Irishman who, as minister for immigration, facilitated Asian immigration to Australia and multiculturalism. So vicious were Grassby's allegations that Barbara Mackay and her family solicitor were responsible for the disappearance and murder of her husband Donald Mackay, who'd had the temerity to contest an election against Grassby in 1974, the entire law of criminal defamation came back to life. After Grassby's death, we learned his Mafia associates included the man who'd ordered Mackay's execution.

So if my books spoke of the wretchedness we white people are and how wonderful is everyone else, I could lie and murder anyone defying me, without people caring. My books don't do that, so I need to be righteous and be seen to be. I can't afford so much as to leave the butter out of the refrigerator. I just can't be self-righteous, for which I would be condemned.

We give up our heroes and heroines for the sake of other races. In 2015, the Connecticut Democratic Party resolved unanimously to strip the names of former presidents Thomas Jefferson and Andrew Jackson from its annual fundraising dinner because of their ownership of black slaves and Jackson's role in the removal of Native Americans in south-eastern America. "I see it as the right thing to do," said Nick Balletto, chairman of the Connecticut Democratic Party. "You can't change history, but you don't have to honour it."

Our opposition to white racism accords us heroes from other races, other people's heroines, sharing our pursuit. In 2013, the American Congress unveiled a statue of black American Rosa Parks, who'd refused to give up her seat for a white man in Montgomery, Alabama, in 1955.

The only memorial not to fallen soldiers or an American president in the National Mall, Washington was unveiled in 2011. A statue thirty feet tall, eleven feet taller than the statues of presidents Lincoln and Jefferson, dominates the four-acre memorial. It honours not a great scientist, writer, or artist, but black America's champion in the face of white American racism: the Reverend Martin Luther King, Junior.

The memorial isn't just for black Americans but white Americans, too. It's for others benefiting from the eradication of white American racism, although I can't imagine them dwelling upon it to the same depth that black and white America do. The statue is a statement of what postmodern America holds dear, and not simply for having been made in China.

A year earlier, in 2010, media commentator Glenn Beck expressed our new, multiracial collective with the words "whites don't own Abraham Lincoln," and "blacks don't own Martin Luther King." Different races together fighting white people's racism have become central to American identity. It's the only commonality we've been able to conjure in our cultural diversity and disparity.

It's not much. Black Reverend Al Sharpton complained of Beck's insensitivity planning a rally to restore honour to America by "honouring our heroes, our heritage, and our future," as well as troops deployed in Iraq and Afghanistan, on the same steps of the Lincoln Memorial (intentionally or not) that forty-three years to the day beforehand King gave his most famous speech: *I Have a Dream.*

Beck had previously accused black President Barack Obama of being a racist who hated white people, but speakers at his rally of predominantly white people were careful to avoid talk of race. Slowly revealing the conflict between our natural human racism and the efforts we make to wipe race from our thoughts, writer Christopher Hitchens, best known for advocating atheism, wrote that the speeches and others like them "deny racial feeling so monotonously and vehemently as to draw attention." He called it "white self-pity," feeling like a persecuted minority when we weren't a minority yet. We aren't meant to complain about anything.

Two decades earlier, in 1990, my American friend Kathy's mother, at home in Connecticut, was never more exuberant than she was the day the white South African government released dissident black leader Nelson Mandela from house arrest. Mandela went onto become president of a black majority South African government. In 2008, Britain celebrated his ninetieth birthday with fervour greater than that for any Briton's birthday, including that of Queen Elizabeth II. In 2012, British comedian Eddie Izzard ran twenty-seven marathons in Mandela's honour, representing the twenty-seven years he'd been detained during South African apartheid.

The first time our youngest children's primary school photographs came in a book was in 2011. It included only one quote ascribed to a person: Mandela. "Education is the most powerful weapon which you can use to change the world," he'd apparently said, twelve years earlier. Given how much we use education to indoctrinate our children, he might've been right.

The last Tuesday of July that year, rugby league coach Wayne Bennett addressed the New South Wales Mineral Industry Health and Safety Conference at the Crowne Plaza Hotel in the Hunter Valley. Having spoken about great moral leadership, he was asked who he thought demonstrated it. Bennett could have nominated his wife or himself, not so much for dealing with professional sportsmen but for raising two disabled children. Instead, he mentioned Mandela, along with Indian nationalist Mahatma Gandhi.

Their reputations for pacifist conflict doubtlessly add to their standing in our eyes, but their racial nationalism being directed against white people doesn't diminish our esteem for them. It accentuates it.

White people the world over practically deified the black Mandela who personified his people's opposition to white minority rule in South Africa, while paying little attention to brave heroics of people like Polish shipyard worker Lech Wałęsa and Czech playwright Václav Havel, who led their countrymen and women's struggles against communism, but never had the chances to help Africans so much. If we want to be heroes and heroines among the wide Western populace then instead of doing anything to help our races, we better help other races. Convening concerts to raise funds for African famine relief earned Irish singer Bob Geldof an honorary knighthood.

The last Sunday in October 2010, Brother Ned invited the congregation at our parish Anglican church to name some wise people. Jürgen mentioned Mandela. Afterwards, I remarked to Jürgen about white people making heroes of black people.

"It helps them lift themselves up," explained Jürgen, without meaning to condescend.

"It hasn't worked."

"No, I know."

"We even made one of them president of America, but it hasn't helped."

16. WHITE IDENTITY

Not only have Jews failed to learn to live around the Holocaust. So have we.

Late in the 1980s, or early in the '90s, a young man in conversation with me wondered why the Liberal Party of which he was a member made so much effort to help Aborigines when few, if any, of them voted for it. "It's not for the votes of black people," I explained, "but for the votes of white people."

We can no longer bear to think of our identity being race, but race remains at our core. Black American academic Janet Helms wrote of a white racial identity in her 1992 book *A Race is a Nice Thing to Have: A Guide to Being a White Person or Understanding the White Persons in Your Life*. She blamed white racism for holding other races back and wanted a positive white racial identity devoted to dismantling the privilege of being white: "*a non-racist White identity*."

We've been letting other races tell us what being white should mean since the Holocaust. Another black American academic, Beverly Daniel Tatum, believed that white people don't identify as being white because we have only three categories from which to choose: colour-blind, racist, and ignorant. Other races aren't so restricted, neither in the West nor elsewhere.

Nazi Germany started the Holocaust. British, Russians, Americans, and other European races ended it. The latter are as much our white post-Holocaust identity as the former.

While a young woman, American educator Ali Michael decided not to bear children so she didn't propagate her white privilege. (I learnt of Michael from my Jewish friend David's comment on the Facebook website: "*I agree it is best someone like that should not breed.*") Race consumes us more in our rejection of racism than it did when we were comfortably racist.

We never lose our racial natures, but ours is the racism of rejecting our own. Citing Tatum, Michael wrote in 2015 that she learnt from the black family in which she embedded herself that *"the job of White people lies with teaching other White people, seeing ourselves clearly, owning our role in oppression… But the lesson for me is remembering how deep the pain is, the pain of realizing I'm White, and that I and my ancestors are responsible for the incredible racialized mess we find ourselves in today… But we cannot not be White. And we cannot undo what Whiteness has done."*

It's a perception that blames all the inequalities in the world, or at least in the West, on white people's oppression of others, now and in the past, while taking on the burden of redressing it: helping other races until they possess all we possess. We have no other purpose.

Trish Crossin had been an Australian Labor Party senator representing the Northern Territory for fifteen years when, in 2013, Prime Minister Julia Gillard summoned Crossin to her office. Gillard told Crossin she wanted her legacy to be an Aboriginal woman in the Australian senate. She was thus organising Crossin's removal from the top of the Labor Party ticket, and her retirement from politics at the next election, to recruit former Olympic hockey player Nova Peris. Peris was Aboriginal. Crossin was not.

At the time, Gillard would have been unaware of Peris' correspondence with Trinidadian athlete Ato Boldon in 2010. Peris wrote, *"this is all black money babe"* of government funding for Aborigines, but *"white people hate black people in this country, and don't like for things to happen if there is no salt in the mix…."* We're the salt.

President George W. Bush received no kudos for appointing Colin Powell America's first black secretary of state in 2001 and Condoleezza Rice her first black woman secretary of state in 2005 because, in the words of an American cited in the *New York Times* newspaper, Bush "never thought about race." Our rejection of racism requires us not to ignore race, but to promote people from other races because of their race.

We're not looking for definition. We think we've already found it. Ours is an ideological identity, the identity we've come to know best. Nothing's more important to us than ideology.

"I think a lot of the problems in the world would be mitigated if he were the face of our country," said white American actor Matt Damon of Barack Obama in 2007. "I haven't ever met him or talked to him, but he's the first person in a long time who I've been inspired by." Obama's talk of bringing America together again was like that of no end of other political candidates, including Bush before his first presidential election eight years earlier, but we remember very little.

On the third Monday in March 2008, the previous Democratic Party presidential nominee John Kerry explained why he endorsed Obama so early in the new round of primaries. "It would be such an affirmation of who we say we are as a people," said Kerry, "if we could elect an African American president." Furthermore, Kerry believed Obama's election would help America relate with Muslim countries. "He has the ability to help us bridge the divide of religious extremism, to maybe even give power to moderate Islam to be able to stand up against this radical misinterpretation of a legitimate religion." The reason was racial. "Because he's African American, because he's a black man, who has come from a place of oppression and repression through the years in our own country."

Religious faith had nothing to do with it. Obama's middle name, a legacy of his Muslim paternal grandfather Hussein, might have helped, but his Kenyan father became an atheist. His white mother (an only child whose parents named Stanley because they wanted a boy) had called herself an atheist since high school.

An African American president, Kerry went onto say, would be "a symbol of empowerment" for people around the world who'd been disenfranchised, "an important lesson for America to show Egypt, Jordan, Saudi Arabia, other places in the world where disenfranchised people don't get anything."

Obama wasn't descended from slaves (as increasing numbers of black Americans aren't, but we don't differentiate between Africans descended from voluntary immigrants and those descended from involuntary slaves. Obama's parents separated when he was two years old, before his mother married another Muslim and took Obama with her to live in her new husband's native Indonesia. Obama spent four years there, presumably franchised. His disenfranchisement certainly wasn't the Punahou School in Hawaii, a private preparatory college he attended from fifth grade (soon after which his mother separated from her Indonesian husband) while living with his mother's parents. Nor was it Harvard University, where he was elected its first Law Review black president.

Kerry called Obama disenfranchised not because of any experience he or his family had suffered, but because he was African in America. His was a victim race.

In an election where the mantra was change, at least one commentator observed that Obama represented change not for anything he promised but for whom (or perhaps the word was "what") he was. As avowedly as we insisted nobody mention his race, we knew what he was. We liked that about him.

Tobin Van Ostern, a junior at George Washington University, led the Students for Barack Obama organisation. A young white man, he saw a black president as "appropriate for the direction the country is going."

We support people from other races because of their race, but complaining about it is racism. "If Obama was a white man, he would not be in this position," said Geraldine Ferraro, who'd been the Democratic Party nominee for vice president in 1988, "and if he was a woman he would not be in this position. He happens to be very lucky to be who he is, and the country is caught up in the concept." The outcry forced her resignation from advising Hillary Clinton's campaign.

While still only a candidate, although assured of the Democratic Party nomination over Clinton, Obama toured Israel and Europe. His deification surged among people knowing even less about him than Americans knew. Pleased to see America, the last of the twentieth-century superpowers, no longer European, our overarching presumption was that America led by Obama would be more peaceful: less likely to intrude.

Two hundred thousand Germans thronged before him at the Victory Column in Berlin the penultimate Thursday in July, giving voice to what seemed like tens or hundreds of millions of Europeans yearning him on. Beneath the golden goddess built for the glories of Prussia more than a century earlier, our messianic vision of an unthreatening coloured future addressed them. Obama did so as "a proud citizen of the United States and a citizen of the world," as we wanted him to be. "The walls between the countries with the most and those with the least cannot stand," he told them. "The walls between races and tribes, natives and immigrants, Christian and Muslim and Jew cannot stand."

His was a perfect statement of our white people's vision of the world, unfolding since 1918 and especially since 1945. We'd have gleefully cut our limbs from our bodies for his benefit.

On the far side of the globe, there seemed hardly a child in my children's primary and high school that didn't share the adulation.

The *Sydney Morning Herald* newspaper was as certain as anyone in the West's rejection of Christianity, while its front-page headline reporting Obama's presidential inauguration, with letters as large as I ever saw in the newspaper, called him the messiah. (Since American films had begun portraying God with black actors and an actress, the assumption was understandable.) So powerless had we become, he was a chance to save us when we no longer believed God or we can save us.

When we support other races because of their race, they're merely a means of us attaining our objectives. In an article titled 'Obama the 'Magic Negro',' *Los Angeles Times* newspaper columnist David Ehrenstein called Obama the latest beneficiary of young white America's pursuit of an idealised, unthreatening black man, who'd heal its deep senses of racial guilt for slavery a century and a half earlier and segregation half a century earlier. Obama's candidacy offered healing to wash away a little of our shame.

The white identity others dictate for us depends upon our ignorance. Young white Americans didn't know fifty-three people died through six days of race riots in Los Angeles only sixteen years earlier. "So a lot of the acceptance and the lack of relevance of race is simply a lack of history," observed Clemson University political scientist Joseph Stewart, an older white Southerner supporting Obama. "We usually think that's a bad thing, but there may be some positives too."

We dwell upon allegations of our ancient racial wrongs, but not the facts of recent days and years. We glean and soon forget the news: the world around us, but for all our dreams of racial harmony and raising other races high, we know our dreams are failing. Something's amiss, but Obama offered daytime for our dreams: a chance to try anew. For dressing and behaving so much like the most urbane of white men, he assured us races could be equal after all.

There was crime and the faces of criminals were disproportionately black, but Obama wasn't about to bash us to the ground. He was the black man we weren't afraid to see near us in a street (as Obama's grandmother had been afraid). We hoped that all those black people, most notably the young men we try not to imagine when we think of crime, might be inspired to be what we wanted them to be: that they'd all don suits like his, go back to school, and become polite and unintimidating. He made us think we could become minorities and everything would stay the same. The gangs we never mention, at least not by race, would dissipate.

Obama won overwhelming majorities of the vote among racial minorities and young white Americans even more than had recent Democratic Party candidates, but only forty percent of white Americans overall. Racial guilt is a luxury for people wealthy enough to afford it. Poor people have less for which to feel ashamed.

Guilt for America's segregationist past motivated white Americans born after segregation ended more than it motivated those alive through its final years. Only a minority of older white Americans voted for Obama. Older people remember history that younger people aren't being taught. For all Obama's talk of removing walls between races, walls between white people remained.

"The election wasn't so much about what Obama brought to the table," said Timothy Johnson, a founder of the Frederick Douglass Foundation, in October 2010. "People voted for him because they wanted to feel good about themselves, that they weren't racist."

By people, he meant white people. The Frederick Douglass Foundation promoted black Republican Party candidates; race remained a cause for loyalty among black people. Johnson was black.

Johnson believed Obama wasn't scrutinised properly before his election because of his race. (We didn't analyse Obama oblivious to race; we didn't analyse him at all.) He also believed Obama set back the cause of race relations by playing down his white heritage. "His mother was white, his father was a person of colour but every time there's a racial issue he plays the race card just the same as everyone else."

American fears of being labelled racist meant Obama could hardly help but be as successful a president as he'd been a candidate. After every spoken error by his predecessor Bush had been endlessly repeated supposedly to prove he was an idiot, Obama's gaffes went unmentioned. I only discovered by chance a month or more afterwards his explanation as to why he couldn't converse with the Austrian president during his first visit to Europe: "I don't speak Austrian."

That's not to say anything against Obama. I wouldn't dare.

Actress Angie Harmon was accused of racism when her concern about unemployment meant she criticised Obama exhorting extravagance during economic recession. She saw the hypocrisy of people applauding Obama for appearing on Jay Leno's television show who would have criticised Bush doing the same.

"A lot of people don't want to feel anti-black by being opposed to Obama," said Ed Asner, former president of the Screen Actors Guild, in 2013, explaining why the actors and actresses who'd so publicly opposed Bush's military actions in Iraq weren't criticising Obama's proposed military actions in Syria. Asner was Jewish.

Ours is no less a racial identity than any other, except that ours is unique for bringing us no comfort or a people or place to call our own. It gives us none of the loyalties other races enjoy. Their identities give them histories to own and cultures to share: the comfort of race.

We abandon all thoughts of our heritage, except when we sense a chance to regret. We dwell in our racial identities, especially our racial histories, when it's a chance to punish ourselves for our race. We obsess with white people's racism and presume other races are poor victims of it. If we're racists, we're most complicit in our forebears' and other white people's wickedness, real or imagined, keeping other races down. If we're against our people's racism, we're absolving ourselves a little from racial infamy. It's our rehabilitation, but never seems to help. We're shamed from liking anything about us.

17. THE RULE OF WORDS

Asterisks now fly in lieu of writing what we widely recognise as being the N-word. As provocation, it excuses all manner of violent replies, but nineteenth-century writer Mark Twain used it candidly without derision. The word was a commonplace colloquialism, slang even, when Negro sounded formal.

Alfred Hitchcock used the word in a rare caption to his 1927 silent film *The Ring*. The black actor can't have been offended, unless we insist he was too oppressed to mention it. If we think he was too oppressed to notice he was being oppressed, then we're calling him stupid.

Simply because we abandoned rules of grammar and spelling doesn't mean our language is without rules altogether. New doctrines replaced them, enforced more harshly than by mere school detention or caning. We've abandoned notions of blasphemy and obscenity in respect of God and morality, but enforce something stricter about race. Words have come to mean so much.

Racist books and nursery rhymes quietly disappeared, becoming news only when schools, preschools, and local councils were so heavy-handed as to declare their bans. "The history behind the rhyme is very negative," said Birmingham City Council when it banned 'Baa Baa Black Sheep' in 2000, "and also very offensive to black people." Without any corroborating evidence, it claimed the rhyme originated from slavery.

A parental backlash overturned the ban in Birmingham, but time was not on the rhymes' side. Six years later, a nursery in Sutton Courtenay banned it.

(Fixated as Birmingham City Council remained with nursery rhymes, it changed the ending to 'Humpty Dumpty' in 2009, presumably to avoid offending eggs. "All the king's horses and all the king's men couldn't put Humpty together again," became "made Humpty happy again.")

In 2011, Pelicans Innisfail Child Care Centre in Queensland

wasn't so crude. Nor was it encumbered by reality (as I suppose 'Humpty Dumpty' wasn't). Catering to indigenous and non-indigenous children with white dolls, darker-skinned dolls, and dolls of both sexes, it also set its sights on 'Baa Baa Black Sheep'. Children began singing about rainbow sheep.

Soon enough, our local primary school did the same. I imagine whole generations of children growing up believing there are rainbow sheep.

Forever yearning for more proof we've rejected our past racism, our language became colourless. The Northern Ireland Human Rights Commission in 2009 removed words that connoted what it called a *"hierarchical valuation of skin colour."* It advised its employees to replace the phrase *"black day"* with *"miserable day."* It counselled them against the term *"ethnic minority,"* which could imply *"something smaller and less important."*

The South West Regional Development Agency was similarly particular. *"Terms such as 'black sheep of the family', 'black looks', and 'black mark' have no direct link to skin colour, but potentially serve to reinforce a negative view of all things black,"* it advised. *"Equally, certain terms imply a negative image of 'black' by reinforcing the positive aspects of white."*

I had to read that last sentence twice. Any language that reinforced something positive about being white needed to be removed, because it implied something negative about being anything else. *"For example,"* the agency confirmed, *"in the context of being above suspicion, the phrase 'whiter than white' is often used. Purer than pure or cleaner than clean are alternatives which do not infer that anything other than white should be regarded with suspicion."*

We don't worry about names like great white sharks. They are sharks, after all.

Contrariwise, the University of California by 2015 deemed language offensive for removing all hint of race. Phrases such as *"America is the land of opportunity"* and *"America is a melting pot"* its faculty training guide labelled *"micro-aggressions,"* because other races could see them *"denying the significance of a person of color's racial/ethnic experience and history"* or telling them to *"assimilate to the dominant culture."* Thus it also objected to the statements *"I believe the most qualified person should get the job,"* and *"Everyone can succeed in this society, if they work hard enough."*

White people must respect people of other races retaining their racial loyalties and sensitivities. Pretending that races don't exist is our supposed white privilege.

Abbreviating words is commonplace, and there was a time a student escaped punishment for referring to an Aborigine in class notes as an *"Abo"* by adding the full stop denoting abbreviation. Not anymore. Melbourne resident Brett Nicholson was thinking of an unrelated acronym when he entered the letters *"abo"* into the Google website search engine in 2010. It brought up an advertisement for tourism in the Northern Territory. *"An experience you'll never forget. Experience Aboriginal culture in NT."*

"I was quite shocked," Nicholson said later. "My initial reaction is to blame it on incompetence. Sure, Aboriginal culture represents massive opportunity for Tourism N.T. and it's clearly a focus for them, but I still think this is inexcusable."

A spokeswoman for Google shared his concern. The company didn't allow offensive advertisements, such as those with racist language. The advertisement itself wasn't.

That evening, I typed *"abo"* into Google. Most results were about the controversy: ninety-eight articles, at least.

I also typed *"Aussie"*, *"Yank,"* and *"Pom"* but found no controversy. New Zealanders can be called "Kiwis" and Englishmen "Pommy bastards" with impunity. They might be citizenry rather than race, but the phrases are only applied to white people. No one's sensitivity stops us from using abbreviations and slang terms for white people, although calling French people "Frogs" and Germans "Krauts" has fallen from fashion. Still, they're not censored from websites, newspapers, or television.

Amidst the furore after former Carlton Football Club president John Elliott referred to Aborigines as "Abos" in 2011, journalist Andi Mastrosavas explained. *"It is the Australian version of America's "N" word,"* she wrote, *"and it has been used historically and routinely to denigrate and demean Indigenous Australians... Terms like Kiwi, Yank and Aussie are innocuous because they refer to powerful, white, dominant cultures. Language becomes offensive when it seeks to oppress... It is not political correctness gone mad to suggest that all members of society should speak to each other and about each other respectfully."*

Not everyone gets such respect. Mastrosavas began her article by labelling Elliott a *"bigot."*

Language became a means to oppress white people. Bigotry, racism, and a forever growing line of phobias torment and ostracise dissidents, until dissent disappears.

Mastrosavas' presumption that past slang terms for other races sought to oppress them flowed from the presumption that everything our forebears did was to oppress other races. It wasn't.

The 1950 Australian and British film *Bitter Springs* was very sympathetic to, even supportive of, Aborigines. Among many Aboriginal cast members, one played a character named Blackjack.

The greatest advocate for Aborigines in the film was a white trooper. "When whites take over Abo land, there's three ways of dealing with the natives," he told settler Wally King. "One, you can shove them off. Two, you can ease them off. Three, you can find some way of taking them in with you."

Mastrosavas' analysis suggested that calling Japanese "Japs" would be racist in Australia but not in Japan, but our linguistic paternalism means we daren't abbreviate the names of other races or anything about them. Japanese are Japanese, with unending respect. With single syllables already, Thais can't be abbreviated, however much Thai food we eat.

Even where white culture is powerless and subordinate, as it is when we're victims of crime, we can't taper our respect for other races. (We shouldn't be mentioning the races of criminals anyway.) "*Couple caddies got rolled by some Pakkis*," wrote golfer Steve Elkington on his Twitter computer account during the 2013 Senior Open Championship in Liverpool, England, "*bad night for them*."

Elkington hurriedly apologised before tournament officials punished him. "*Being Australian, I was unaware that my use of language in relation to the Pakistani people would cause offence, but having been made aware I now deeply regret the use of that terminology*."

More than a million computer messages in 2012 mentioned American-born basketball player Jeremy Lin. China claimed him as its own. White America was even more enraptured with him. Black American boxer Floyd Mayweather, Junior was rude enough to point out the reason. "*Jeremy Lin is a good player but all the hype is because he's Asian*," Mayweather complained on the Twitter website. "*Black players do what he does every night and don't get the same praise*."

Mayweather was roundly criticised, as if he were white. "*Other countries get to support/cheer their athletes and everything is fine*," he wrote later Monday. "*As soon as I support Black American athletes, I get criticized*." Later again, he wrote: "*I'm speaking my mind on behalf of other NBA players. They are programmed to be politically correct and will be penalized if they speak up.*" Racial politics was never more complicated.

"Chink in the armour" had been a commonplace phrase. Editor Anthony Federico had used the word "chink" hundreds of times over the years without anybody caring, until he posted a headline after Lin's mistakes caused his team to lose a game to New Orleans. *"Chink in the Armor: Jeremy Lin's 9 Turnovers Cost Knicks in Streak-Snapping Loss to Hornets."* ESPN immediately fired him.

"The C-word is for Asian Americans like the N-word is for African Americans," explained California congresswoman Judy Chu, claiming Federico's use of it was no error but deliberate. "The word was used since the 1880s to demean Chinese Americans and to deprive them of rights, and it is used on playgrounds specifically to humiliate and to offend Asian Americans. So I don't know where he's been all this time." She dismissed Floyd Mayweather as the "heavyweight champion of insensitive remarks."

With our great sensitivity to race, we encourage others to be sensitive. We can hardly blame them for taking advantage, even if our indulgence doesn't assist them.

In 2013, Jieh-Yung Lo threatened to involve the Human Rights Commission in demanding that Team Bondi change the name of a planned computer game *Whore of the Orient*, an historical nickname for the city of Shanghai. "Whore" wasn't the word about which he complained. "It's the use of the word 'Orient' more even than the word 'whore' that is the issue," he explained. "The O-word is very similar to the N-word for African American communities. It's a nineteenth-century racial colonial conception and it's especially painful for older people in the communities."

Lo cared about his elderly. He also cared about his ancestors, calling the game an "attempt to disgrace Chinese culture, history, and traditions."

Lo had no qualms about disgracing British culture, history, and traditions. (Neither do we.) Nine months earlier, after being elected to the national committee of the Australian Republican Movement, he said the Queen was "old-fashioned" and "irrelevant" to Australians.

No longer is there even a third party collective pronoun regarding another race. The second Monday in August 2011, my eldest daughter's year-eight geography teacher asked the class a question something like, "What would happen if the U.S.A.

economy failed?"

The teacher wrote her answer about the Chinese, beginning "*They...*" A moment or two later, she realised her error. Apparently not wanting any sense of separation between her geography class and the Chinese, she replaced the pronoun with "*The Chinese...*"

In 2012, the owners of a Victorian racehorse named their horse after artist Charles Blackman, but somebody complained the name Blackman could be interpreted as Black Man. Myles Foreman, the chief executive of the racing registrar, said the name "could be construed as being offensive." (It wasn't necessarily offensive, but could be so construed.) The registrar consulted with the owners to "ensure the wrong connotation could not be taken." The owners renamed their horse Lady Blackman.

We don't mind racial epithets about white people. "*A recent absurdity was an Irish woman's use of racial vilification laws to prosecute her neighbour for calling her a leprechaun,*" wrote zoologist Rob Morrison in 2011. "*Sensibly the case was dismissed as 'political correctness gone mad'.*" Political correctness goes mad when white people try to rely on it.

The only point of his semantics was changing people's attitudes. "*If we are to counteract ethnic, religious and other forms of discrimination... surely we need to identify their root causes clearly and use precise terminology to describe them. They have different causes needing different solutions. If you hate Jews or Muslims, you are not a racist but a bigot. If you fear foreigners, you are not racist but a xenophobe. Calling someone a leprechaun is not racist, but politically incorrect.*"

In practice, we call a racist a bigot, even if we call a person a bigot for other reasons too. A xenophobe is racist because the only times we care that people fear foreigners are white people fearing foreigners from other races. We don't call people xenophobes for fearing white people.

If our opposition to racism were simply protecting the powerless from the powerful, we'd not have worried about American-born Solomon Trujillo. Awarded one of Australia's most sought after jobs, the head of public company Telstra, he brought with him two Americans: Greg Winn (who would earn twenty-one million dollars for three years employment) and a cantankerous government relations man Phil Burgess. They quickly became known as "the three amigos," for which nobody admitted any inspiration but the film *The Three Amigos*. It nevertheless teetered too close to Trujillo's parents being Mexican for many people's liking.

Endlessly sparring with the company's largest shareholder, the Australian government, Trujillo became deeply unpopular with investors, customers, and employees alike for his brashness, arrogance, and the deep decline in the company's performance and share price through his tenure, well before the global financial crisis set in. He left in May 2009 having been paid thirty-five million dollars, earning more money in four years of failure than other people earn through lifetimes of success.

"Adios," said Prime Minister Kevin Rudd.

"*Adios, amigo, to the man who enfeebled Telstra,*" headed Ian Verrender's *Sydney Morning Herald* report.

A newspaper cartoon portrayed Trujillo as a "*sleepy-eyed sombrero wearing clichéd Mexican,*" in the words of marketing expert Stephen Downes. "*Regardless of what you think of the job Trujillo has done at Telstra or of his bonuses and golden parachute arrangements, the use of racist imagery to depict anyone should be just as unacceptable in Australia as it is in the US.*" Rich and powerful as he was, we should have treated Trujillo as an individual without race, while fretting for poor, powerless Latinos.

For his part, Trujillo told the British Broadcasting Corporation that Australia was "like stepping backward in time," but it was only so in the West. He criticised racist, backward Australia for having relaxed our immigration laws only thirty years earlier, most likely unaware and certainly unconcerned that countries outside the West had never relaxed theirs.

"*What do you think of Trujillo's comment?*" asked the *Sydney Morning Herald* computer poll, offering only three possible answers: "*Australia is racist and backward,*" or "*Australia is neither racist nor backward,*" or, for which I voted, "*Sol is backward.*" There was no option for Australia being racist and not backward, or being backward and not racist.

"*Sol, your wake-up call is important: we've no good reason to be smug,*" headed journalist Adele Horin's response. She acknowledged Australians were much less racist than people in other countries, but remained unsatisfied. "*If they do not fulfil the multicultural fantasy of becoming best friends, or inter-marrying, they are civil and helpful to one another.*" She wanted us doing even more, picking out incidents of racism as a cause for her crusade.

In particular, Horin complained that the previous Australian government had questioned the value of multiculturalism, going so unforgivably far as to imagine some priority for British traditions. "*Lack of political leadership unleashed the incivility and racism that usually lies dormant.*" Western political leadership demands keeping racism dormant.

Of the same race as Trujillo was Sonia Sotomayor. Only a few days later, her nomination to the American Supreme Court entailed no end of talk of her race, but she was a success. We can speak of other races when something's good about them.

18. THE SERIOUS MATTER
OF HUMOUR

We worry about every spoken word, determined not to be racist. Racism is much too important. "There can never be an appearance of racism or bigotry in any high position of leadership," declared Massachusetts senator John Kerry in 2002.

That didn't deter him from jokes disparaging Europeans. "The Iraqi Army is in such bad shape," he quipped on the Don Imus radio show, "even the Italians could kick their butts."

We laugh at the supposed stupidity of New Zealanders with names like Ian and Craig (as were two separate jokes I received by electronic mail in August 2008) and Irishmen, even if American jokes about Poles have gone from the public eye. Commenting upon jokes as a pervasive example of bigotry against white people might seem trite, but jokes about other races aren't.

Barack Obama was a candidate for the Democratic Party nomination in 2008 when Colorado businessman William Farr addressed the National Western Stock Show's annual Citizen of the West banquet. Preparing to read a telegram from the incumbent president's official residence, the White House, he joked, "They're going to have to change the name of that building if Obama's elected."

"I gasped," said Governor Bill Ritter, sitting at the table with Farr.

We don't need to know anyone of another race feeling offence, although it helps. "I think it was uncalled for and atrocious," said Hispanic senator Ken Salazar.

Farr meant no derision, but the uproar from people offended at any mention of Obama's skin colour was heard around the world. We treat jokes about colour most seriously because we're very serious people. Farr apologised no end.

We can at least laugh at ourselves. More than anything else, we need to laugh.

Jokes about white people's skin colour are perfectly acceptable, as they were about Obama's Republican Party opponent in the 2012 election, Mitt Romney. "Well, as you know," host Jay Leno said on an episode of the *Tonight Show* in February 2013, "there is a, oh my God, just a huge snowstorm going on back east... You know, I spoke to my buddy in Boston. They've already gotten a ton of snow in Boston. He said Massachusetts is now whiter than a Romney family reunion."

(Romney's family might've felt the insult. Later that year, his son Ben adopted a black baby.)

We can mock whiteness to our hearts' delight, but can't even allude to other races. We focus our attention upon jokes, because most people aren't powerful enough to practice any other discrimination. It would be petty if we thought racism was petty and boring if we wanted to laugh, but laughing can be particularly distasteful.

Stevie B, presumably a model, from Vancouver may well have been defending herself from a charge of racism when, on the last Friday of April 2012, she typed a message through the Twitter website for the *Gloss* website. *"Making a joke about your friend being black doesn't make you a racist any more than standing in a garage makes you a car."*

Of all the oppressions inflicted upon people who might otherwise be free, the cruellest have been those stripping humour from our lives. The safest course is not to say or do anything referring to someone of another race, as Danish tennis player Caroline Wozniacki discovered during an exhibition match in Sao Paulo in 2012. She impersonated black American Serena Williams by stuffing towels into her bra and pants. Wozniacki didn't blacken her skin, but critics saw something racist about a voluptuous figure. Any hint of race is all our offence requires.

We're no more forgiving of private conversations than public addresses. In May 2013, rugby league commentator David Morrow thought his conversation was private when he joked about the darkness in Darwin meaning dark-skinned people only became visible when they smiled, but his words were erroneously broadcast to faraway Wollongong. The Australian Broadcasting Corporation suspended him from commentating, pending an investigation.

Kevin Dunn from the University of Western Sydney, lead researcher in the Challenging Racism project, considered it irrelevant whether Morrow intended his comments to be hurtful or that he was unaware they were being broadcast. "Morrow's assumption that his comments are okay in the private sphere indicates there are still some challenges in confronting racism in Australia."

We're supposed to cease racism with or without an audience. Nobody need suffer, nobody need know, but we still call it wrong. The joke can be inside our heads, but our heads we are trying to change. Not merely should race never be alluded to jovially. Hidden away in the recesses of unimaginable minds, it shouldn't be treated lightly.

At the end of November 2013, Cricket Australia removed another Australian Broadcasting Corporation employee, ground announcer David Nixon, after he introduced English-born Monty Panesar to the crowd at a match in Alice Springs with what someone thought mimicked an Indian accent. Nixon denied the allegation, but what sounds or appears racist is racist. Two days later, he still hadn't meant anyone who thought he'd introduced Panesar with an Indian accent, but we need only one person alleging racism for the allegation to stick. Speaking with what sounds like an Indian accent is racially insensitive.

The jokes we can make are those about work, wealth, and values: lawyers, aristocrats, and people whose political opinions aren't ours. I think it might've been the *Law Society Journal* that suggested lawyers had become the butt of so many jokes because jokes about other races and religions had become impossible. We can joke about racists, but not about race. Well, other races anyway.

We still have white people to mock. Finding humour from current events, the Australian television programme *Good News Week* made mention of Scotswoman Susan Boyle, whose beautiful renditions of songs like 'I Dream a Dream' had made her the darling of other white people forty-seven years old, like me. "Of course, she's ugly," callously quipped a young, attractive blonde comedienne on the panel. "She's Scottish!"

The audience laughed, and Channel Ten must have assumed the extract would draw viewers by including it in the advertisement for the show on the Queen's Birthday Monday, 2009. It didn't draw me; Boyle appearing on the programme might've drawn me. I simply noted how unimaginable would be calling any race not European ugly.

The sense of humour we've lost when it comes to any slight

upon other races finds full voice and eager audiences when deriding our own. Caroline Wozniacki, then the world's leading female tennis player, admitted to making up her story of being attacked by a kangaroo during a visit to a wildlife park while in Melbourne for the 2011 Australian Open tournament. She called her instant of stupidity, "a blonde moment." No hair but Western is naturally blonde, or unnaturally blonde to any obvious degree, so we can stereotype blonde people as stupid.

There was none of the outcry that would later follow her impersonation of Serena Williams. There was no outcry at all.

"Our girls are very smart and they have degrees," insisted blonde Giedre Pukiene, the managing director of Lithuanian company Olialia, in 2010. "All of them want to do something with their lives. They have lots of business ideas." She announced the company would establish a holiday resort in the Maldives staffed by blonde people, which readers of the Maldivian news service Minivan condemned for being discriminatory against Maldivians. (Nobody complained about Maldivian laws requiring at least half the staff at resorts to be Maldivian.)

Red-haired people are also uniquely European. Michelle Griffin, arts editor of the *Age* newspaper, explained that remarks about rangas aren't akin to racism because they're doing pretty well, at least in the West. "*Are redheads barred from the top jobs in the land?*" she asked. "*Obviously not… They appear to be doing well in business…, in the media…and sport… Are redheads considered ugly? …The beauty industry has always had a thing for redheads… Even in the 19th century, the red-haired beauty was still celebrated: the pre-Raphaelite muse…*" If redheads want immunity from being derided, they should commit more crimes or cease earning money. "*Redheads are not over-represented in our prison populations, or below the poverty line.*"

Prohibiting discrimination against other races hasn't validated their mockery as our lack of any restrictions upon red-haired people is supposedly reason to joke about them. "*There are no immigration quotas for the red-haired; they're paid the same as blondes. No religions fulminate against them; no politicians revile them. There's anecdotal evidence that redheads are easy marks on the playground, but this isn't backed up by any findings in the serious research into bullying.*" (We don't undertake research, serious or otherwise, into bullying of white people.) "*Redheads get called redhead names, but they don't catch half the grief of the overweight, the disabled, the poor or the foreign.*" We dismiss talk of harm to ordinary white people because we think everyone else suffers more.

We're not about to accuse Jews of racism. From what I saw and heard of it, British Jew Sasha Baron Cohen's 2006 comedy film *Borat: Cultural Learnings of America for Make Benefit Glorious Nation of Kazakhstan* revealed the desperate efforts white Americans make to be polite to even the rudest and stupidest of foreigners, tolerating antics they wouldn't tolerate from each other. Yet critic Kirk Honeycutt saw only Americans' hypocrisy and bigotry when referring to the film in his review of Cohen's next film *Bruno*, which denigrated Austrians.

Other races don't joke about themselves. They joke about us.

My elderly Chinese friend Weston was a frivolous character, excitedly repeating jokes he'd heard others say. "A blonde and a brunette jump off a building," he told me, the first Thursday in July 2007. We have no problem with a joke about suicide, when both jumpers are white. "Who reaches the ground first?"

I guessed the brunette because, in blonde jokes, the blonde is an airhead. I was right, but for the wrong reason.

"The brunette," confirmed Weston, "because the blonde stopped halfway to ask directions."

After laughing, he proceeded into a second joke, much the same as the first but without anyone dying. "A blonde with an economy-class ticket sat in the first-class section of a 'plane," he said. "She refused to leave, until someone whispered in her ear. After she left, he was asked what he had said to make her go. He replied, I told her that the first-class section isn't going to Melbourne."

Other people's racism doesn't excuse our racism. Nothing does that. Ours is the racism we're determined to destroy.

With our support behind them, those other races aren't as jovial as we are to hear jokes about them. In 2011, the ambivalence of Asian Americans to the American military led some to question whether multiracial America could ever defend her interests in Asia, but the American Army's focus wasn't fighting America's wars. It was fighting American racism, even if it's just making jokes. *"Everyone here jokingly makes fun of me for being Asian,"* wrote Private Danny Chen in a letter to his parents. Two days later, he wrote: *"People crack jokes about Chinese people all the time; I'm running out of jokes to come back at them."* In October 2011, he killed himself.

Quick to blame those jokes instead of anything else in Chen's life, Asian groups wanted the American soldiers prosecuted. Just two months later, which was a very short time for the American Army to prosecute soldiers, it obliged. Training its weapons upon racism, the army charged eight of its soldiers with various offences including manslaughter and negligent homicide.

Our frenetic obsession with racism meant a hundred Victorian police were caught up in a scandal for having sent or received an electronic mail message considered racist early in 2010. The force demanded Tony Vangorp explain why he shouldn't be dismissed, after being a policeman for thirty years. The third Friday in March, forty-seven years old, he resigned rather than be fired. The following Monday, while collecting his personal belongings from his desk at Healesville police station, the father of two adult children shot himself dead.

Another well-respected father of two was medical technician Roy Amor, sixty-one years old. A month after Vangorp's suicide, Amor noticed an immigration official outside the Opcare clinic at Withington Community Hospital, Manchester. He joked to a black friend that the colleague "better hide." His friend wasn't offended, but another colleague overheard him and lodged a formal complaint. After thirty years' service without facing any disciplinary proceedings, Amor was suspended from work for five days while a disciplinary investigation was carried out. Fearing he'd lose his job, Amor shot himself dead.

We love to exhort the power of one when the one defied our past racism. When the one defies our present rejection of racism, defying our demagoguery, we're merciless. He or she is a freak when few of us are freaks. We're the righteous lynch mobs, hanging the one we call racist from a tree.

In 2016, after chatting with an Asian boy through their computers, sixteen-year-old English schoolgirl Phoebe Connop shared with her friends a photograph of herself with her skin darkened and wearing a scarf wrapped around her head. That, she said, would be her requirement to get approval from the boys' parents. Her comment was about their racism rather than hers, but when the photograph was shared beyond her friends, she feared Asians calling her racist. Thus, she hung herself.

Not everyone cares. In response to the story of Amor's death, Niger_man of Nigeria wrote, "*Well, it WAS racist.*"

19. ACCEPTABLE
AND UNACCEPTABLE ABUSE

Within fifty years after Menzies' proud declaration, another Australian prime minister never contemplated being British. Paul Keating called his long-dead predecessor an Anglophile, as if that were an insult. He enjoyed deriding older Australians who still respected Menzies or harked back to anything good, as he never derided people from other races feeling the same for their histories. Keating's entire engagement with Asia seemed predicated upon not any affection for Asia but his antagonism to Britain, for he never drew comfort from being Australian. His predecessor Bob Hawke quoted him calling Australia, "the arse end of the earth."

Since we ceased being racist and became individuals, we've become more and more abusive. We swear and blaspheme without compunction as our grandparents couldn't imagine. We tear each other down over anything. Hell, we love abuse, but one whiff less than respectful of other races and we recoil with gut-felt offence.

The innocence of youth means we normally expunge children's criminal records when they reach eighteen years of age (as most infamously occurred for the young murderers of James Bulger in England), but American journalist Tracie Egan Morrissey, writing as Jezebel, thought youth allowed no relief for racism. She wanted teenagers who'd described Barack Obama as a "*monkey*" on the Twitter website after the 2012 presidential election punished for life.

President Obama was more powerful than were any of those teenagers and probably unaware they'd made their remarks, but Morrissey reported them to their school principals and superintendents. She published their details, intending to maintain that public computer record where anybody searching their names would find it, prejudicing their future study and job applications. Morrissey was white.

The only people free to use derogatory racial epithets are those at whom those epithets were once directed. Uruguay-born Rosanna referred to herself as a "wog," but objected to our friend John then doing so. They were two of the four people, two couples, who recruited me into our local Neighbourhood Watch before leaving.

A decade later, in 2010, rugby league footballer Dean Young allegedly called opposing player Robbie Farah a "f***ing wog" during a game, although some witnesses claimed he'd said "f***ing dog." Calling him a dog would've been fine.

"To call the Lebanese-background Farah a 'wog' is not only an ethnic misfire," wrote journalist Malcolm Knox, *"but it harks back to a time when people of Mediterranean, that is Italian and Greek, origin were routinely vilified."* (Knox was younger than I was and we attended the same school, where I recall only one mention of wogs.) *"Yet they, like the nigger-speaking African Americans, have reclaimed the word with gusto... It's hard to see what sense 'wog' carries nowadays. Perhaps all it carries is the primitivity of Young's anger."* (I wish I could invent words like primitivity and dispropriating.) *"Farah didn't take exception, other than, by his own admission, to try to use it to milk a penalty. The NRL, in finding that Young did not have a case to answer, acted with common sense. Young might be stupid, but the content of racial vilification in his alleged words is unclear."*

Abuse without racism isn't really abuse. Racist abuse we call vilification, often making it a criminal offence.

Other races racially abusing each other are problematic. Knox acknowledged *"it's hard to know what to make of them,"* after mixed-race Maori and Aboriginal rugby league player Timana Tahu called a sixteen-year-old boy a "black c***" during a competition reserved for indigenous Australian footballers at Woy Woy. *"Where it's one black man abusing another, the matter is complicated. Indeed, there's been a great tradition of dispropriating language from the oppressor and neutralising it, such as black Americans calling each other 'nigger'. In their mouths, it is not vilification. In a white mouth, it is. The retrieval of the word is brilliantly empowering, but it all depends on who is uttering it and to whom."* (We think nothing's more brilliant than other races becoming empowered.) *"If the allegations against Tahu are correct, he wasn't using the word in that brotherly sense. But it's not the same as a white player using it... Tahu ought, if the allegation is correct, to be sanctioned for bullying, but not necessarily for racial vilification."*

The previous June, Tahu quit the New South Wales team because he'd heard Andrew Johns describe Queensland player Greg Inglis with the same phrase he later used against that sixteen-year-old boy. He responded to criticism of his abuse by telling a television interviewer, "My own people are out to get me." His people were Aborigines like his mother, that day.

Other days, his people were Maoris, as they were when he played in the New Zealand Maori team to honour his late Maori father. Mixed-race people find it hard to know who their people are; Aborigines didn't see him as theirs.

Early in 2011, the jovial presenters of the British television programme *Top Gear* were discussing a sports car built in Mexico. "Cars reflect national characteristics, don't they," remarked Richard Hammond. "So German cars are very well built and ruthlessly efficient, Italian cars are a bit flamboyant and quick, a Mexican car's just going to be lazy, feckless, flatulent, overweight...leaning against a fence asleep, looking at a cactus, with a blanket with a hole in the middle as a coat." By the end of his words, he was laughing aloud.

"It is interesting, isn't it," responded James May, "because they can't do food, the Mexicans, can they, because it's all like sick with cheese on it, I mean?" He too laughed.

"Refried sick!"

"Yeah, refried sick."

"I'm sorry, but just imagine waking up and remembering you're Mexican: 'aw, no'." Hammond laughed.

"No, it'd be brilliant...because you could just go straight back to sleep again."

The furore in Britain was immediate, although I was most interested by comedian Steve Coogan's critique. He'd cleverly lampooned conservative white men as much as radio and television interviewers in *Knowing Me, Knowing You, with Alan Partridge*, one of the two or three funniest television series I'd seen, but never lampooned other races. He'd appeared on the *Top Gear* programme, but no friendship with the hosts was going to moderate his condemnation.

Coogan began by saying the *Top Gear* hosts wouldn't label kosher food as looking like "*sick with cheese on it*" or describe Islamic fundamentalists as lazy and feckless because those groups were too well organised. Mexicans, at least in Britain, weren't. (British people can be the most organised, but we're defending other races.)

The British Broadcasting Corporation's defence of the *Top Gear* hosts didn't impress Coogan. "*It cited the more benign rivalry that exists between European nations (ah, those arrogant French, over-organised Germans), and in doing so neatly sidestepped one hugely important fact – ethnicity. All the examples it uses to legitimise this hateful rubbish are relatively prosperous countries full of white people. How about if the Lads had described Africans as lazy, feckless etc? Or Pakistanis?"*

Abusing Europeans is acceptable. Abusing other races isn't.

Coogan reacted to a negative generalisation about Mexicans by making a positive generalisation about them and a negative generalisation about middle-class white Americans. *"I can tell you from my own experience, living in the US, Mexicans work themselves to the bone doing all the dirty thankless jobs that the white middle-class natives won't do."*

Middle-class people the world over, including in Mexico, didn't do those jobs either. Middle-class white Americans employed poor Mexicans instead of poor white Americans.

"If I say anything remotely racist or sexist as Alan Partridge, for example, the joke is abundantly clear. We are laughing at a lack of judgment and ignorance. With Top Gear it is three rich, middle-aged men laughing at poor Mexicans. Brave, ground breaking stuff, eh?

"There is a strong ethical dimension to the best comedy. Not only does it avoid reinforcing prejudices, it actively challenges them."

Coogan went onto make a string of cutting jokes at the expense of those three rich, middle-aged men. For reasons unclear, he then added to his derision, *"the National Rifle Association in the US who, I'm sure we can all agree, are a bunch of nutters."*

Were the members of the National Rifle Association not primarily white, his abuse and stereotyping of them would presumably have been unethical. Our ethics don't demand that we challenge prejudices against white people.

The third rich, middle-aged man to whom Coogan referred was Jeremy Clarkson, who attracted further controversy in 2012 for his solution to long queues for border control checks at Heathrow airport. *"Nobody is waved through anymore,"* he wrote in the *Sun* newspaper. *"The result is plain for all to see. There's a two-hour wait, and the problem is: the only possible solution is to introduce a bit of racism."* His tolerance of racism was still very low. *"Nobody likes a racist. Nobody likes prejudice. It has no place at work, at play, or in government, but at Heathrow airport? Hmmm."*

Clarkson became specific. *"You can't get that sort of thing past the bleeding-heart liberals. They believe that…a hook-handed imam with fire in his heart and hatred in his eyes is just as likely to whip up anti-western sentiment as Joanna Lumley,"* a popular, delightful English actress.

Uproar again followed, although nothing so eloquent as Coogan's had been the previous year. A spokesman for the Public and Commercial Services Union, which represented Border Force workers, said simply, "Clarkson is an idiot."

That was relatively temperate aside the abuse we wield upon younger, poorer white racists. In February 2012, the Finke Desert Race Grid Girl modelling competition expelled teenager Ellen Musk because of her derogatory comments, away from the competition, about Aborigines. Labelling her "white trash" was inescapable irony, but we've made racists the rubbish of our race like nobody else.

Class is never too far away. We only call poor racists our trash.

We again became hysterical in November 2012 after passengers on a Melbourne bus abused a foreign woman who started singing in French. "Speak English or die," mattered more than, "Everyone on the bus wants to kill ya."

We're not to abuse other races. We're to abuse our own. Journalist David Penberthy described his country, Australia, as *"a nation of uncouth bastards."* He wanted the racists on that bus gaoled for the rest of their lives. (Jewish journalist Joe Hildebrand only wanted them gaoled for twenty or twenty-five years, as a message against racism.)

Journalist Peter Munro made all manner of derogatory generalisations about people who ride on buses unimaginable about other races or religions. *"First, bus riders are not lovers or fighters. They're loners, skilled in the art of ignoring strangers, masters of the sideways glance and muttered voice."*

People on buses, trams, and trains didn't used to be loners. We spoke to each other, before interracial immigration.

Sportspeople and spectators feel the passion about sport we only know to express with abuse, but ordinary or even extraordinary abuse doesn't bother us. Players are tough enough not to let people think it affects them, unless it's racial.

Among the first cases brought before the Australian Football League judiciary was Todd Curley allegedly addressing David Cockatoo-Collins as "you black c**t." Curley explained that he had called him a "weak c**t." He was acquitted of any offence.

That C-word seems to be the abuse of choice among

sportsmen. Also that year, 1997, Michael Prior proved to the tribunal that he'd called Robbie Ahmat a "dumb c**t" instead of a "dark c**t" by repeating each phrase while wearing the mouthguard he'd worn during the game.

At the time I was working for Holyman Limited. Reuben, the finance director, told me he thought being called dumb was a bigger insult than being called dark. Apparently, it wasn't. We rush to condemn racial vilification without concern about stupidity vilification.

Spectators can also be sanctioned. Not only did Nigerian-born Gold Coast player Joel Wilkinson object to racial abuse from a Collingwood supporter in June 2012, so did white Collingwood player Dale Thomas and fellow Collingwood supporters, who the club said were "deeply offended." The supporter agreed to write letters of apology to everyone affected, but within forty-eight hours after the abuse, Collingwood terminated his membership of twenty years. We have no loyalty to racists. (We have no loyalty to anyone.) The club would only consider his application to rejoin after he undertook a racial vilification re-education programme.

Adam Goodes was a strong, successful footballer thirty-three years of age, who never flinched from the physical contests his sport demanded. Like other footballers, he'd heard no end of abuse from partisan spectators and opposition players. He also wore a beard, which was the reason a thirteen-year-old schoolgirl, in the crowd watching the Sydney game against Collingwood in May 2013, called him an "ape." Unfortunately for her, Goodes was Aboriginal.

In any other case, a man thirty-three years of age responding to the words of a girl thirteen years old would be pathetic. It might even be bullying her, but not with racism. Goodes pointed her out to authorities who evicted her from the grounds.

"Hopefully the police have got the person," said Collingwood president Eddie McGuire afterwards, "and we'll find out and get to the bottom of it." Police interviewed the girl and released her, while McGuire vowed to seek out the girl and ban her from the club. It all dominated the Australian news, and not simply the sporting news, that night and the next day (while five nights of immigrants rioting in Sweden remained unreported, as far as I saw).

McGuire himself fell victim to our fixation with racism the following Wednesday, during his breakfast radio show with Luke

Darcy. McGuire was presumably looking for every opportunity to say good things about Goodes when Darcy mentioned a promotion for the musical *King Kong* in Melbourne. "Get Adam Goodes down for it," interjected McGuire, "you reckon?"

"No, I wouldn't have thought so," replied Darcy.

McGuire later apologised. "I was that exhausted this morning," he explained.

Much as McGuire wanted the girl removed from football, journalist Anthony Sharwood wanted McGuire removed from radio. The Australian Football League sentenced McGuire to its racial and religious vilification policy.

Ironically, the Sydney game against Collingwood that previous Friday night was the first of the games making up the indigenous round that year, which the Australian Football League described as *"a celebration of our country's Indigenous culture and players that have shaped Australia's Game."* We'd made race central to that weekend of football, and were furious when a thirteen-year-old girl forgot.

20. WHITES-ONLY RACISM

When Daisy Hernandez, a former editor of *Color Lines* magazine and an editor of *Colonize This! Young Women on Today's Feminism*, heard a man had shot Arizona congresswoman Gabrielle Giffords and killed several bystanders in Tucson in January 2011, her loyalty was racial: to prospective immigrants from Latin America. She wanted to know the killer's surname, fearing a Latino assassin would lead to tighter immigration controls (although past killings by immigrants hadn't). "My eyes scanned the mobile papers," she told National Public Radio. "I held my breath. Finally, I saw it: Jared Loughner, not a Ramirez, Gonzalez, or Garcia. It's safe to say there was a collective sigh of brown relief when the Tucson killer turned out to be a gringo."

Gringos are white people, but the West doesn't pillory other races for their racial derision. The words and people offending us are ours.

Through the early 1990s, I think, I saw a television interview in which a black American woman defined racism as being white people's attitude to other races. By definition, she said, only white people could be racist.

In 1998, the Australian television programme *Media Watch* demonstrated journalist Jana Wendt's lack of professional skills by scornfully broadcasting an extract from her programme *Uncensored*. After a black South African said his father considered white people (who ruled that country until 1994) amoral, Wendt cautiously asked him, "Was he a racist?"

Rationalising a similar attitude was Bahar Mustafa, the welfare and diversity officer at the Students' Union of Goldsmiths, University of London in 2015. Welfare means helping races that aren't white. Diversity means removing the white people. Mustafa organised university events banning white people and men, referred to "*white trash*," and called through the Twitter website for people to "*kill all white men*." She insisted that "I, an ethnic minority woman, cannot be racist or sexist towards white men because racism and sexism describes structures of privilege based on race and gender, and therefore women of colour and minority genders cannot be racist or sexist because we do not stand to benefit from such a system."

Mustafa had benefited very well from a white people's system that helped her live, work, and organise in Britain as no race outside the West allows, but she had no sense of being helped or even allowed to do so. "In order for our actions to be deemed racist or sexist," she explained, "the current system would have to be one that enables only people of colour and women to benefit economically and socially on such a large scale and to the systematic exclusion of white people and men, who for the past four hundred years would have to have been subjected to block colonisation. We do not live in such a system. We do not know of such a history."

Why four hundred years, I don't know, but given the way we pore through history interpreting our past heroism as misdeeds while ignoring other people's misdeeds against us, even making them heroic, we can hardly criticise other races doing the same. Block colonisation had already made Englishmen and women minorities in much of London and Europeans are becoming minorities in much of the West, but that was immaterial. Mustafa assumed that white men had spent four centuries systematically holding other people down and were still doing so, although I found no complaints from her about men of colour. Her complaints about gender were in the context of her complaints about race. "Reverse racism and reverse sexism are not real."

We agree. Only other races are victims of racism. Whatever white victims are, we're not victims of racism.

Among the comments supporting Andi Mastrosavas' criticisms of Australians abbreviating the names of other races in 2011 was from Cloud Strife, a particularly intriguing moniker. "*The newer definition, as taught in uni, of racism is prejudice plus power. A white person in a white dominated culture can be racist. A POC in a white dominated culture can be prejudiced, but not racist.*" It took me a moment to realise that in our new regime of politically acceptable abbreviations, P.O.C. means person of colour.

The new definition raised several provocative ideas, all of them academic. (We tend to think anything academic is unimportant.) Aside from Jews, Europeans are the only races on earth widely accused of racism, in spite of us being the only races to admit other races as immigrants. The best way then for us to help other peoples isn't by admitting them into our countries but by leaving them in their own, where their systems and cultures dominate. Excluding immigrants by their race isn't racist, because they never become subject to our white-dominated cultures.

In reality, we are not so nuanced. People of colour aren't racist in their countries however they treat us or any other race, because we insist ours is the dominant culture on earth. If theirs is racism then it's innocent racism. Even if we realise we're no longer so dominant, we'd need four hundred years suffering under other races before Bahar Mustafa would consider other races racist. By then, we'd have rationalised another reason that only white people are racist.

Other races agree. The people claiming they cannot be racist because theirs is not the dominant race are not saying racism depends on power in places they are the dominant race.

The abuse of power is not in racism. It is in the prejudice against racism. It is power we grant other races over us.

Focusing on power should mean that poor and powerless white people could not be racist, but they are the people most mocked for their racism. They suffer most from our rejection of racism.

We treat our national borders as expressions of white power, to be unwound in pursuit of equality. Other races can have borders. Equality is only for the West.

The International Cricket Council banned Australian cricketer Darren Lehmann from playing in a series of five one-day international games for calling Sri Lankan cricketers "black c**ts" outside their dressing room in January 2003, but not because Sri Lankans are brown. (Cricketers aren't less abusive than footballers, not anymore.) The council seemed less concerned about black men attacking white farmers in Zimbabwe, which was among three African countries hosting the coming World Cup. We've made words more important than rape and murder, when the words are white racial abuse.

A short time later, Pakistani cricketer Rashid Latif called Australian cricketer Adam Gilchrist a "white c**t," but abusing white people isn't racism. (Not abusing racist white people would be.) We accept people hating us.

Australian sports journalist Patrick Smith explained, quite

sincerely, that white people calling black people "black c**ts" was racist because it validated our supposed systematic persecution of black people through history. Smith didn't specify that persecution, which was so validated by one man casting abuse outside a cricket team's dressing room in 2003. I doubt Smith knew anything more than I knew about British colonial rule in Sri Lanka, although at least I knew the country was then called Ceylon. Smith brought all dark-skinned people into one grand group of European victims. Racism is for whites only.

What we don't ignore, we excuse, exonerating other races from racism when they racially abuse us. If this is our racial punishment, then we punish our futures for what we now deem the failings of our past.

Another journalist to condemn Lehmann was Malcolm Knox, who in 2010 refused to condemn a Sri Lankan player who'd denigrated Australians as sons of convicts. Knox equated the distinction to not feeling offence if his brother called him a "spaz," but being furious if he'd used the term to describe a spastic. *"The point,"* wrote Knox, *"is that vilification of any kind is not just a matter of a word: it's all to do with context… But words of race aren't just words. They are loaded with history. As white people in Australia have not been subject to invasion, dispossession, marginalisation and a host of other discriminatory behaviours and policies, it's as hard for me to take legitimate offence from being called a 'white c***' as it was to be called a 'spaz'. There is no history of abuse, in Australia, carried by the word 'white'. When it comes to the word 'black', there are 222 years of it."*

White people now suffering dispossession because of immigration can't expect such understanding. Nor does anyone care when we experience discriminatory behaviours and policies in countries outside the West. Events before we were born (well, some events anyway) mean we can't relax our rules about race. Other races' loyalty to their ancestors who supposedly suffered so much at our ancestors' hands (the people we think we were) becomes admirable; we understand their righteous abuse. What we think are the crimes of our long racial past require retribution.

In Knox's view, the insurmountable burden of history carried by white Australians pales aside that carried by white South Africans. *"As for a South African swimmer describing an Indian spectator as carrying on like a monkey, that's a different matter altogether. Both the term of abuse, and the speaker, carry so much history on their backs that it's more like a gorilla.*" (Knox was writing before a little girl got in so much trouble for calling Adam Goodes an ape.) "*Roland Schoeman had a fair point in reacting to unruly fans at the Commonwealth Games swimming, but before he spoke he might have given more thought to what country he comes from, what country he's in, and how their respective histories had brought them here. If anyone was the racial buffoon of the week, it was big Roland. But he escaped with no more censure than the lettuce-leaf flayings of the Indian media.*"

Schoeman had been provoked by the abuse he'd received from Indians in Delhi. Neither Indians nor we cared that Indian was the dominant culture there.

We'd screamed against white South African racism through the time of apartheid, but aren't so fussed about African tribalism: racism coming closer to home. In 2012, David (the head of the parents and citizens association at my eldest son's high school) told me of his experiences in black-dominated South Africa after apartheid ended. An African doctor, trained in Harley Street, London to help Africans, entered an operating theatre dressed and prepared to undertake surgery, but took one look at the patient from another tribe and turned around. "I'm not operating on him," he said.

Our vision of a West beyond race often clashes with our embrace of other races, but we only struggle when the clash offends other races. While serving on the board of our children's preschool early in March 2006, Father Keith told my wife the school was suffering a newly arrived Chinese immigrant who insisted her child not be in a class because the teacher Sheelagh, an Australian-born Indian, was dark. She was adamant that dark-skinned people could be servants but not teachers, at least not for her child. Teaching white children (including our second son) was fine, but not teaching Chinese. Furious that the school would not immediately accommodate her, I could well imagine her complaining of bias against Chinese.

The discussions we think can resolve any conflict never did. The Chinese woman got what she wanted, while the school apologised profusely to the teacher.

Neurosurgeon Charlie Teo being keynote speaker for Australia Day 2012 wasn't remarkable; the Australia Day Council wasn't going to let the controversy a year earlier around him auctioning tickets for people to watch him operate on cancer patients keep it from selecting so successful an immigrant, particularly one appearing regularly on television. Nor was there anything remarkable about him complaining about Australia racism, in spite of the career he'd enjoyed in supposedly racist Australia. "It's very difficult for people who aren't of Asian appearance to say that there's no anti-Asian sentiment... You've got to really be in their shoes to make statements like that."

What was remarkable was Teo's admission, tucked well down in the news report of his award, that other races are racist too. "Chinese, for example, are very racist," he said. "Some of the comments my mother made when she came out here first would surprise you."

It was the first media mention I'd read of anyone but white people being racist, although it passed without comment, at least that I read. We're normally not so racist as to mention the race of a racist.

The *News Limited Network* in October 2012 included the headline: 'Aussie flees Singapore after racist Facebook rant.' The woman in question had complained about a noisy Malay wedding being conducted below her apartment late into the night. "*How many f*ing days do Malay weddings at void decks go for?*" she wrote. "*Pay for a real wedding...maybe then the divorce rate won't be so high. How can society allow people to get married for 50 bucks?*"

Nobody cared about her vulgarity. All anyone cared about was her racism. She lost her job at the National Trade Union Congress for Membership, Partnership, and Alliance, and, following threats of violence against her and family, fled Singapore. The racist we called Australian was Malaysian-born Chinese woman Amy Cheong.

Our companies are no less culpable than our countries for other people's racism. The following month, November 2012, Jae Ladd complained through the Twitter website, "*@British-Airways F*** you. F***in cancelling my flight! #bunchofc**ts.*"

Only someone knowing Ladd or seeing a photograph of him would know he was Asian. "*Go back to your f***ing country you gook,*" came the reply from British Airways.

The airline hurriedly apologised, but amidst the condemnation of the airline, it was immaterial that its representative who'd sent the reply was Gordon Qiu. "*its a joke,*" claimed Qiu, "*lool hes my friend.*"

Other races aren't so fearful of being labelled racist as we are.

They don't feel the insult.

What then is racism? Racism is white people thinking or feeling about race the way that people of other races remain free to feel and think about it.

When only white people are racist, then fighting racism is fighting white people. Eradicating racism is eradicating white people.

If only white people are racist, then the whole concept of racism becomes intrinsically racist. It's racist post-racism, in response to which we wage our racist anti-racism. That fundamental inconsistency, that illogic, should be reason enough for the white racist stigma to abate. It hasn't been so far.

21. THE PRESUMPTION
OF WHITE PEOPLE'S RACISM

"People rub along in a benign way," said Macquarie University researcher Amanda Wise of suburbs with a polyglot of races in 2009, satisfied with a fairly low standard of the best those suburbs can be. "The problems are in white areas like Sutherland Shire where people have no contact with cultural difference and form stereotyped views."

There's presumably no problem in black, brown, or yellow areas. The problem is us.

I'm not sure where Wise formed her stereotyped view of white people living in white areas. My friend Peter, a finance manager with whom I worked, lived in the Sutherland Shire, but refused to vote for an overtly racist political party. He thought refugees shouldn't be forced to return to their homelands when the reason for their refugee status ended; spending time in the West was reason enough for them to remain. His positive views of other races flowed from having no contact with them.

Surely some English blood flowed through Peter's Irish veins, but he unabashedly explained his reason for wanting Australia to become a republic, "I just don't like the English." Neither Wise nor anyone else cared about people disliking Europeans.

We can't make any more negative stereotypes of white people than to call each other racist. It's our favourite stereotype, and it presses us to do more to eradicate racism.

Writing for the *Daily Telegraph* newspaper in 2009, journalist Joe Hildebrand put together a funny and vicious mockery of actor and director Mel Gibson titled 'Cute, Crazy, Catholic,' while generally applauding Gibson's film-making. (His mockery of the Roman Catholic Church was less funny.) One particular sentence struck me, and not simply for embodying the juxtaposed compliment and derision throughout the article. *"For it is a sad truth that many people in the non-racist, non-sexist and non-homophobic community cannot see past Mel's Aryan quirks to the courage and heroism contained in much of his work."*

I read the sentence several times trying to understand it. In spite of white people being the only people on earth no longer racist, sexist, or disapproving of homosexuality, Hildebrand deemed them Aryan quirks, although he acknowledged those attitudes are natural. *"Human beings are simply animals,"* he wrote, *"it's just that some of us have evolved further down the line than others."* The others are presumably Aryans.

The West doesn't particularise Aryans anymore, not since the Holocaust, but Hildebrand wrote elsewhere that he was Jewish. (He has also said that he wasn't.) Born in America before being raised in Australia, Gibson was of Irish stock, without German or other Aryan blood in him, but to be racist is to be Aryan in the most pejorative terms. Racism becomes a white person's quirk.

The accusations of Gibson being racist flowed primarily from a drunken anti-Semitic rant a few years earlier, although Gibson and several of his friends and colleagues, including some Jews, denied he was anti-Semitic. Gibson had been accused of intolerance of homosexuality for the depiction of a weak, sexually ambiguous Prince Edward in his 1995 film *Braveheart.* I don't know what about Gibson was sexist, although it might've been marrying, siring seven children, separating, and then siring an eighth with a new girlfriend. Perhaps it was just being Roman Catholic.

When the *Associated Press* news service reported racial conflict in Paris, Texas in July 2009, it referred to *"black separatists"* and *"white supremacists."* Without evidence to warrant the distinction, we presume white people caught up in racial conflict are supremacists while blacks simply want space. (What we call separation, the rest of the world calls countries.)

The weapon of choice through the world through recent years has been to call white people racist. The R-word swiftly and single-handedly overwhelms all other considerations. Certain that race poisons everything a racist thinks, nobody should listen to what that person says, or care what that person feels.

People of other races unhappy with anything we do or aren't doing need only accuse us of being racist: the button to make us do or not do what they wish. No amount of their racism need deter them; it doesn't deter us. We're far too fearful of being called racists to call people of other races racist, and provoke the racist barb in reply.

Having insisted that we consign our baby son's pram to the cargo hold for our aeroplane flights from Adelaide to Melbourne and then Sydney in 1997, Ansett Airlines mislaid it. Late that Sunday night, standing with me at the baggage counter in Kingsford Smith Airport, Sydney was a distraught Australian whose luggage had also gone missing, but the aging East Asian behind the counter was of little help to any of us. The Asian didn't care about the Australian and his luggage, while his poor knowledge of English made him particularly useless. Becoming increasingly frustrated, the Australian asked how things were done in "your country?"

Any last notions of customer service, rather poor to start with, completely evaporated. "You're a racist!" snapped the Asian. Every time the aggrieved customer tried to speak, the counter attendant cut across his words, refusing to listen. "You're a racist," he said more angrily, his voice rising with a passion he hadn't bothered to feel for the passenger's lost luggage. His knowledge of English was never better than it was each time he said it. "You're a racist!" We've let words become weapons.

A few years afterwards, Ansett Airlines collapsed. If it wasn't the lost luggage, it might've been the customer service.

Surveys talk of Australia being a racist country, but that includes people quick to describe their countrymen and women as racist without considering themselves racist. (It's hard to imagine such surveys being undertaken outside the West.) When other races complain they're suffering discrimination, it means white people again.

They don't need to complain. They need only be mentioned.

In 2013, Australian football attracted smaller crowds than soccer games in Western Sydney. "We don't have the recruiting officer called the immigration department," explained Greater Western Sydney coach Kevin Sheedy, "recruiting fans for Western Sydney Wanderers."

Soccer analyst Craig Foster described Sheedy's comments as "*a disgrace to this country*" and "*a throwback to the dark old days of anti-immigration.*" He told Sheedy: "*Talk of your past work with any non-Anglos, anything. Camps, coaching sessions, travel, anything you can come up with. Just show you are not a racist old Aussie with no concept of the Australia of today.*"

Sheedy had a long record working with indigenous people.

"When I said the immigration department was one of the best recruiting agencies for soccer," he responded, "well I didn't mean anything untoward by that, but it's a fact." Facts are the problem. "Racist is a pretty broad term.... I think people just get a bit touchy on certain things, and I'm not touchy in that area at all."

Most of us are; we want to make our best impressions. Fear of the accusation of racism being uttered against us paralyses whole Western populations.

In 2013, a royal commission heard two victims testify to the profound effect child sexual abuse by former scoutmaster Steven Larkins had on their lives. The next day, former regional commissioner Allan Currie testified that Scouts Australia did not dismiss Larkins, who'd been caught showering with the victims and putting love notes under their doors, because it feared "he could then use the racial discrimination card." Larkins was part Aboriginal.

Tensions simmered for years at Cronulla Beach in Sydney, with Lebanese abusing and threatening to rape the "Aussie sluts" wearing bikinis, before a group of Lebanese bashed some volunteer lifeguards in December 2005. Lebanese rushed in from other suburbs to defend their people (as other races but ours do) while Australians defended their sand and soil (as our governments no longer do), resulting in race riots. "*All Arabs unite as one,*" cried one text message among Lebanese gang members, "*we will never back down, the Aussies will feel the full force of the Arabs. Destroy everything, gather at Cronulla December 18 at midday – spread the word. Together exterminate the enemy at Cronulla. Send this to every lion of Lebanon.*"

Listening to an Australian government-owned radio station one morning during that time, I heard a programme hostess accept without question the tales of racist abuse allegedly suffered by Lebanese at Cronulla. Normally, word of mouth is mere hearsay and a weak form of evidence, but not in matters of race. She sighed at the appalling behaviour alleged of her countrymen and women.

Some mouths carry more evidentiary weight than others carry. When an Australian called to complain about suffering racist abuse from Lebanese, the radio hostess laughed. Specifically, the caller complained that Lebanese derogatorily called Australians "Skip," deriving from a four-decades-old Australian television series broadcast around the world, *Skippy the Bush Kangaroo*.

Instead of accepting the caller's claims of Lebanese racism, as she'd accepted claims of Australian racism, the radio hostess demanded detailed particulars of precisely who'd said what to the Australian and when. When he couldn't provide them to the detail she wanted, she fobbed him away. We trust impeccably the words of others, but expect white people to say whatever lies suit them. The Australian caller's claims that he'd suffered racial abuse from Lebanese seemed only to affirm in the radio hostess' mind that he was another white racist. Accusing other races of being racist is racist.

A report prepared for the New South Wales government criticised police and talkback radio hosts for inflaming the situation at Cronulla. The report presumably offered no criticism of the programme hostess to whom I'd listened.

Four years later, the man tiling our bathroom wall remarked about the only time he'd broken a bone. One evening long beforehand, five men had been threatening Jono's friend. Jono intervened to protect him, when the tallest of the five men said dismissively to Jono, "You're a f***ing Skip!"

Jono was willing to leave, unconcerned about the abuse, but the tallest man among the five prepared to hit him. Jono hit him once, knocking him over. Unwilling to continue a fight they'd lose, his friends led the tall man away. The incident remained unrecorded without any crime reported to police, unless the tall man and his friends complained about Jono. He hadn't said anything inflammatory to them at the time but to explain the racist reference against him, Jono told me, "They were wogs." They were Middle Eastern.

The law caught up. So opposed are we to racial discrimination, we surrender our old legal principle: the presumption of innocence. Since 2008 in Australia, when a complainant alleges racial discrimination in matters of employment or housing, the onus is on the employer or landlord to prove his or her thoughts weren't racist, with documentary or other evidence: our white person's burden of proof. In allegations of white people's racism, there's a presumption of guilt.

The law is predicated upon only the accused knowing the thoughts inside his or her head, but the same can be said of a person accused of any crime. If that demonstrates the special seriousness with which we treat racism, then we must treat it as being more serious than murder or rape. People accused of those crimes retain their presumptions of innocence. The prosecution must provide evidence of their intentions, their *mens rea*.

It's much the same in America. At seven fifteen the second Friday night in October 2007, the Carmike 14 Theatre in Dover, Delaware screened the film *Why Did I Get Married?* Cinema manager David Stewart asking the audience to silence its mobile telephones and be quiet might've been unremarkable, except that the crowd was ninety to ninety-five percent black. Someone complained that Stewart's request implied black people didn't know how to behave in a cinema, whereby he returned to the cinema and apologised, explaining the announcement was company policy. After the film, he waited at the exit door to thank patrons for attending.

That wasn't enough, not with the director of the Office of Human Relations, Juana Fuentes-Bowles, in the audience. (By human relations, we mean race relations.) Fuentes-Bowles didn't just declare she was offended. She organised patrons to file complaints with the Human Relations Commission in Delaware. (Race relations were a business she was drumming up.)

The commission felt the film was "minority themed." (I wasn't sure what that meant, although all the principal cast members in the film were black. Perhaps when whites are a minority of Americans, all films will be minority themed.) The cinema had brought in extra security guards that night who were double-checking tickets, which the commission considered no reason to think less of the patrons' race but evidenced the manager's racism. The commission decided the manager's tone in making the initial announcement had been condescending: it "insulted, humiliated, and demeaned" the patrons. There'd thus been racism in violation of the Delaware Equal Accommodations Law.

The commission ordered the cinema to pay every complainant fifteen hundred dollars, a fine of five thousand dollars, and twenty thousand dollars in plaintiff attorney fees and costs. However cheap the film might've been to make, it was very expensive to screen.

The burden to prove we're not racist can be hard to overcome, but not always impossible. In that case, the cinema was eventually able to discharge its burden. The Delaware Supreme Court overturned the commission's orders, deciding there'd been no racism because there'd been no racist language, no single group singled out, and the announcement had been made to all sessions for which all tickets had been sold.

Incredibly diligent in avoiding racist offence, we're quick to pounce when somebody fails. During the 2012 Olympic Games, America's National Broadcasting Company television network broadcast an advertisement for its upcoming comedy series *Animal Practice* showing a monkey performing gymnastics. Purely by chance, the commercial followed Bob Costas' report of African American Gabby Douglas winning a gold medal for, of all things, gymnastics. Angry viewers immediately accused the network of racism. The network hurriedly apologised.

The report about Douglas had made much of her race. "There are some African American girls out there," said Costas, "who tonight are saying to themselves: 'Hey, I'd like to try that too'."

We need to be excruciatingly careful. Before the papal election in March 2013, the British Broadcasting Corporation tweeted on the Twitter website: *"LIVE VIDEO: Chimney of Sistine Chapel as #conclave votes for #Pope – will smoke be black or white?"*

Not paying much attention to the proceedings of the parliament in which he sat, David Lammy linked the tweet from his account. *"This tweet from the BBC is crass and unnecessary. Do we really need silly innuendo about the race of the next Pope?"*

Lammy was unperturbed when first told the Vatican marked the elections for a new pope with smoke rising from the Sistine Chapel chimney. White smoke meant a new pope had been chosen. Black smoke meant he hadn't. (That's something the Vatican will need to change.)

"It's the juxtaposition of Pope and black and white," responded Lammy. *"But maybe I'm just weary of the endless discussion of race."*

I'd not realised we'd had any discussion about race, but a mention a year or two earlier can seem endless when people want no mention at all. Lammy was black, married to a white woman.

An hour or so later, Lammy must've realised he'd offended someone. *"Note to self: do not tweet from the Chamber with only one eye on what you're reading. Sorry folks, my mistake."*

If ever there was a person without premise to presume white people's racism disadvantaged blacks (instead of advantaging them), it was Lammy. Some years earlier, while appearing on the *Celebrity Mastermind* television programme, he'd been asked which monarch succeeded Henry VIII to the English throne. "Henry

VII," Lammy guessed. At the time, he was minister for higher education.

22. REVERSE RACISM

There can hardly be a more ubiquitous chant than our chant of diversity at every opportunity. Potters (including Nikki, who taught my eldest daughter pottery) convened an exhibition of their works in September 2012 titled *Diversity*, blazing from brochures in a variety of colours and fonts with the caption: "*n. The quality of being different or varied.*" We think mere difference is quality.

Underpinning our talk of diversity is diversity in people, which we evoke most passionately in matters of race. Unable to bear hearing that word, we speak of diversity or cultural diversity. We mean racial diversity.

The end of white racism didn't end our discrimination, however much we insist otherwise. When the *North Shore Times* newspaper wanted a photograph of two St Ives junior girl guides moving into their new hall in August 2014, the photographer (the guides' regional membership officer) rejected white girls for wearing sashes with their badges sewn in the wrong places but not the Asian girl. She gave that girl another sash. She changed not the girl, but the uniform.

There comes yet another Western paradox regarding race. By celebrating diversity, we tacitly acknowledge races are real, for a little while at least. If race didn't matter, we wouldn't notice.

Ours isn't a culture of diversity. We welcome only certain diversities; we don't want racism. There's no diversity when it comes to white people's views about race. Diversity is no more or less racist than homogeneity but instead of being merely a matter of taste, we demand diversity while being hostile to any hint of our racial homogeneity. Diversity doesn't extend to the politics and principles that have become our identity.

Preferring a multiracial populace means we believe our countries are better than they used to be for no other reason than accommodating other races, our cities better for their races no longer being ours. Whether we're among a dozen or a dozen million people, we'd rather be around other races than only ours.

For two of us to be diversity, then we deliberately desire the other person to be from another race. If he or she isn't, then we must wish we were.

Diversity is not about them. It's about us. We're not celebrating other races but ourselves: that we're no longer racist. Adopting for our individual selves mantras of moral superiority, every foreign face to which we smile, foreign hand we shake, generosity to foreign lives we bestow, is our gloating that we've come to be great. We're patting ourselves on our backs and kissing each other fondly for not being the people we were. We think we've advanced not just above other white people inferior to us (with their racist failings we merrily deride) but other races with their racist flaws. We think that makes us better than they are.

We've thus great hope for what the planet will be. We claim to lead the world and insist that we don't: no less self-absorbed than people celebrating their race. All we celebrate about us is our new-found conviction that Europeans are no better than others, but by refusing to espouse diversity for other races' countries, clubs, and suburbs, we're calling our race worse. We prefer a European and non-European to two Europeans but not to two non-Europeans. We reject our race because we reject our racism. We don't like our race at all.

We don't grant everyone equality of opportunity, confident that the equality of races will lead to an equality of outcomes, because it hasn't so far. Through the second half of the twentieth century, American companies, governments, councils, and universities introduced minimum quotas for ethnic minorities; well, the coloured ones anyway. The only racial quotas and other discrimination we countenance are those favouring other races. They must, of necessity, disadvantage ours.

Sonia Sotomayor's nomination to the American Supreme Court brought to light the 2009 case of *Ricci v DeStefano*. The court, by a single-vote majority, held the City of New Haven, Connecticut had breached the Civil Rights Act of 1964 by refusing to certify the results of promotion examinations that would have elevated white firefighters but no black and only one or two Hispanic firefighters, because it wanted higher representation of racial minorities among senior ranks. Sotomayor wasn't yet a judge, but joined Judge José Cabranes, a fellow Puerto Rican, in criticising the majority judges that lacked the courage of their racial convictions.

Sotomayor was right to appreciate racial preferences. Commenting on the *Now! Hampshire* website, Cardinal Hayes '71 was among those rebuking the folklore that Sotomayor had overcome the adversity we assume other races suffer at the hands of our racism. (Websites reveal all sorts of rare insights that are never otherwise mentioned.) *"She grew up solidly middle class... To her credit, she and her brother took advantage of opportunities open to them. The truth is while white girls with similar background and SAT scores were directed toward nursing school, Sonia was given open access to Princeton. This says nothing about her Supreme Court qualifications, it is just the way it was in NY in the 1970's (and today from what I hear)."*

While public universities in California were barred from using race as a factor in admitting students, University of California was three times more likely to accept black students and twice as likely to accept Asians in the 'maybe' category in its second round offers than equally qualified white applicants from 2006 to '09, according to Tim Groseclose, a political science professor there. Black applicants whose family incomes exceeded a hundred thousand dollars per annum were twice as likely to be accepted as Asian and white children whose families earned just thirty thousand dollars and had similar test scores, grades, and essays.

It followed student protests in 2006 demanding more minority students. The university's chancellor met with Groseclose and other members of the university's admissions oversight committee and urged them to find a means of increasing racial diversity. The university denied Groseclose's claims.

"I think this is common – not just the racial preferences, but also the lying," said Groseclose in 2014. "Within academia, there are just certain things you must say are true, even if you know they're false."

Other races aren't a single generic group. Affirmative action favours some races more than others, so Asians are its loudest opponents. Lacking our senses of obligation and equality, they're not as eager as we are to disadvantage their own to help other races.

In 2015, the Chinese–American Association of Orange County, California, the Global Organisation of People of Indian Origin, New York, and the Pakistani Policy Institute, New York were among more than sixty Asian groups in America filing a complaint with the civil rights offices at the American Departments of Justice and Education alleging Harvard University engaged in *"systemic and continuous discrimination"* against American Asians during its admissions process, referring to racial quotas or racial balancing benefiting other races. Yet, twenty-one percent of students at Harvard were Asian.

The racial equality we pursue is one by which white people aren't faring better than other races. We can fare worse.

For all our Western democracies decrying discrimination *against* other races, we're willing to discriminate *for* them. (Even if people of other races aren't victims of white people's racism, they could be.) We call it positive discrimination, as if it were good, or reverse racism, presuming that racism means favouring our own, but it's still discrimination and racism. When any mention of either is distasteful, our euphemism for a euphemism anyway is affirmative action. We call it equal opportunity because it's not, but we'll support anything that speaks of equality. Our post-racial discrimination discriminates against our own.

In a short documentary exhorting diversity I saw around the turn of the new millennium, a white American businessman accepted discrimination favouring other races because, he thought, he'd been the beneficiary of institutional white racism, without explaining what that was. Presuming white people to be unfairly politically and economically powerful, we think being white makes competing merely on merit intrinsically unfair. We don't want advantage, so accept disadvantage.

In spite of bowler Jason Gillespie being Aboriginal, journalists Tim Elliott, Erik Jensen, and Ellie Harvey lamented that in 2009 there was *"something obviously white about the Australian cricket team."* They accused the game's administrators of failing to follow England and South Africa in tapping into what they called *"rich pools of ethnic talent."*

Raj Natarajan, president of the India Sports Club, blamed racism for there being so few "ethnic stars," in spite of Cricket Australia operating a Culturally and Linguistically Diverse programme by which Pakistani Usman Khawaja played for New South Wales. "The administrators can't get past thinking that anybody but a white Anglo guy with blond hair should be in the team."

"South Africa is a bit ahead of us here because they have had a policy of fast tracking people of colour," acknowledged Damien

Bown, general manager of game development for Cricket Australia. "We select people on merit." Selection of people on merit hinders our drive to diversity.

Merit only comes into it within races. The discrimination we want isn't so much against us individually. It's against other white people.

Amidst our arrogance, powerful white people think we don't need anyone's help. We recognise other races to help them, and our own to excuse us from responsibility to help. We're not so racist as to care about white students, contractors, and candidates whose attributes or experience would've entitled them to success but who fail because of our discrimination. They're the people disempowered, while we empower everyone else. We punish powerless white people, because other white people enjoy so much.

The poor of other races have their race and us to help them. Our poor aren't the beneficiaries of anyone's prejudice; no one's aiding them. We presume their poverty and suffering are within their control; they too could succeed and be rich but they've squandered their chance, their privilege being white. Aristocrats and public company boardrooms demonstrate the world is for white people, meaning that poor white people have no excuses. They're the trailer park trash, with only themselves to blame.

Poor white people in collapsible homes don't feel their racism is to blame for people of other races not joining country clubs or failing to become partners in major accountancy firms. They don't feel the problems of the world are their fault, as powerful white people do.

Between our rich and our poor, our middle classes share the arrogance and despair. Ours is a racial response to racial inequalities, advancing racial equality by bringing our people down along with other races up. The rich of other races becoming richer at the expense of our poor means their races become richer and ours become poorer, but no number of poor white people or rich other races keeps us from feeling our wealth is a racial privilege. We sacrifice white people poorer than we are to prove it.

We sacrifice each other, until we're sacrificing ourselves. Hofstra University sociologist Gregory Maney welcomed white Americans like him becoming a minority. "And basically that's going to create pressure to desegregate predominantly white areas," he said in 2008. "Can ethnic minority groups translate their greater numbers into greater political and legal power to challenge systemic discrimination in housing?"

Systemic discrimination is difference we've not overcome. No one bars other races from living in white areas, to the extent white areas remain, but we blame white people because other races want to live together, as we no longer do, or can't afford to live where white people do. The opportunities from the change coming are theirs.

From 2013, the American Department of Housing and Urban Development implemented an Affirmatively Furthering Fair Housing rule. Its database, rolled out in 2015, categorised every American neighbourhood by its proportions of white, black, Asian, and Hispanic residents. Wherever the department found black people too far from transport, good schools, good hospitals, parks, and supermarkets, it would threaten local authorities with forfeiting federal grants and lawsuits for housing discrimination if they didn't improve black proximity. It would pressure municipalities to change zoning laws to allow construction of more subsidized housing in affluent, white areas thereby assisting racial minorities (but not poor white people) to move there.

"It's not just having people of different colours live together just to do so," insisted Dedrick Muhammad, senior director of the economics department at the National Association for the Advancement of Coloured People, in 2013. "This kind of integration strengthens economic equality."

Equality costs. The department estimated compliance costs alone at from three to nine million dollars a year.

By 2015, the Federal Housing Finance Agency, headed by black former congressman Mel Watt, was putting together a National Mortgage Database Project with sixteen years of racial data about bank lending. The Consumer Financial Protection Bureau would investigate lenders for racial bias.

Racial diversity is for white areas. Plastered to look like the Chicago flag on the Bow Truss coffee shop in Pilsen late the last full weekend in October 2015 was the message: "*White people out of Pilsen!*" Pilsen had become predominantly Hispanic.

White poor, uneducated, and other vulnerable are the fodder for our drive to racial equality. By 2013, the number of American households living in poverty headed by white mothers had risen to equal the number headed by black mothers. There were twice as many poor white people as black people.

In 2008, Harvard University economist David Cutler reported a decline in life expectancy of about a year for less-educated white American women from 1990 to 2000. Average life expectancies among other races and groups rose.

From 1990 to 2008, life expectancies fell by four years among white Americans without high school diplomas, according to research published in 2012 by gerontologist Jay Olshansky at the University of Illinois at Chicago. "The good news is that there are fewer people in this group," said Olshansky, drawing comfort from the shrinking numbers of white Americans. "The bad news is that those who are in it are dying more quickly."

By 2008, average life expectancies among white women without high school diplomas had fallen five years, below similarly uneducated black women. Hispanics lived longer than both groups.

Whatever's happening around us, collective racial identities remain. Columbia University black professor Patricia Williams argued that bias against white people wasn't a problem because, in 2011, white Americans remained the most affluent people on earth. She measured wealth by racial totalities; the richest or poorest individuals weren't part of her thinking. We can be destitute and alone, but still be accorded the burden of being so rich a race. Malcontent white people don't understand.

Closing her *New York Times* article with the words, "*A house divided cannot stand*," she saw the division between black and white America, but I was struck by the division within white America. Even if white Americans weren't the most affluent people on earth, we'd find races worse off than we are and help them. We care more for other races than we care for each other. Ours is a powerlessness perversely foisted upon us by race.

If whites were the most impoverished people on earth, we'd look into our past, see how well our forebears did, and give more. We'd find the worse off among other races and help them rather than be so racist as to help each other. Nor would we be so racist as to notice more powerful and affluent races unwilling to discriminate against their own in favour of others. We're recompensing other races for our past ruling so much of the world. A future dominated by other races creates equality across human history. We don't lament our racial fall. We welcome racial equality.

Put simply, there's no friend we won't abandon, crime we won't tolerate, home we won't surrender, or lifestyle we won't sacrifice to prove our unyielding abhorrence of racism. We'd rather slip into multiracial decay than head racist empires. We're damned proud of our decline, but who else will help other races?

23. A GENTLE TOUCH
OF RACISM

Learning to live around the Holocaust does not mean forgetting the Holocaust. It means remembering everything else.

"Be confident in your heritage," President Barack Obama told the historically black Howard University, Washington, graduation ceremony in May 2016. "Be confident in your blackness." I could say the same to white people of our heritage and whiteness.

Obama went onto tell those black graduates, "we have to not only question the world as it is, and stand up for those African Americans who haven't been so lucky..., but we must expand our moral imaginations to understand and empathise with all people who are struggling..., and yes, the middle-aged white guy who you may think has all the advantages, but over the last several decades has seen his world upended by economic and cultural...change, and feels powerless to stop it. You got to get in his head, too."

Our new Western ideals can be no less individually self-interested than the self-interest we condemn in others. We redistribute happiness from other white people to ourselves, while immigrant waiters bring us our hors d'oeuvres. We remain indifferent to our compatriots' loneliness, vulnerability, and despair. Our causes don't include their craziness, misery, or fear, although we'll comfort other races every time.

Africans, Asians, Arabs, Jews, Islanders, and other races are loyal to their own. Why can't we be?

When poor Malays rioted against ethnic Chinese and Indian economic power in Malaysia in 1969, killing hundreds of people, the Malaysian government didn't abandon them. It introduced the New Economic Policy, which included racial quotas and other laws discriminating in favour of Malays against other Malaysian citizens, primarily Chinese and Indian. (While we protested white South African apartheid, we weren't bothered about Malaysia mandating discrimination.)

Without our convictions of equality, other races in countries they inherited don't feel as we feel. They enjoy their privilege, without feeling the passions about racism in their countries we encourage them to feel in ours. Unconcerned about their economic or political dominance, they don't object to their race's racism because theirs is the dominant culture.

Inherited white privilege is simply being white in a country that used to be. In a world that for a time white people dominated, it's simply being white.

Within a fortnight of Britain's National Children's Bureau issuing its guidelines for eradicating racism in 2008, the Equality and Human Rights Commission chairman Trevor Phillips (of Guyanese descent) complained that British television programmers remained "hideously white." He acknowledged that there were other faces on television, but not enough of them. *The Vicar of Dibley*, for example, was specifically criticised for being "all white," notwithstanding that the fictional Dibley was an old English village or that, away from the programme, the star of the show, Dawn French, was married to a black man. They later divorced.

Other races like to see their own. They're not so keen on seeing us. A 2006 study found the British television series *Midsomer Murders* to be "*strikingly unpopular*" with racial minorities.

Among the series' creators was producer Brian True-May, who credited its success to employing only white actors and actresses. "We just don't have ethnic minorities involved," he told the *Radio Times* magazine in 2011, "because it wouldn't be the English village with them. It just wouldn't work… Ironically, Causton (one of the main centres of population in the show) is supposed to be Slough, and if you went into Slough you wouldn't see a white face there. We're the last bastion of Englishness and I want to keep it that way… I'm trying to make something that appeals to a certain audience, which seems to succeed."

He had no qualms about storylines: racial homogeneity with sexual plurality. "If it's incest, blackmail, lesbianism, homosexuality…terrific, put it in, because people can believe that people can murder for any of those reasons."

The programme's commissioning broadcaster, Independent Television I.T.V., promptly responded, but only to his remarks about race. "We are shocked and appalled at these personal comments by Brian True-May," said a spokesman. "We are in urgent discussions with All 3 Media, the producer of *Midsomer*

Murders, who have informed us that they have launched an immediate investigation into the matter and have suspended Mister True-May pending the outcome." White people can't prefer to cast and watch actors and actresses from our races as other races can.

Time and again in our postmodern West, when we mix talk of equality with identity, equality gives way to power. We submit to the ever-growing demands of other races, because we think resisting them would be racist: racial conflict, reminiscent of the Jewish Holocaust. Demands for inclusion of others by us give way to others excluding us.

In October 2019, Sheffield University Students Union banned white students from two anti-racism focus groups. The "*Union want to make a change from being simply non-racist to actively anti-racist*," explained women's officer Rosa Tully. Campaigns against racism are thinly veiled campaigns against white people.

Two months later, Sheffield University began paying twenty students more than nine pounds an hour to be "*race equality champions*." They policed other students saying "*microagressions*," being anything, however minor and unintentional, offending minority groups.

No amount of loyalty and belonging among other races inspires us to loyalty and belonging among ours. Indifferent to their discriminations against us, all that matters is that we don't discriminate. It's our racial anti-racial identity, not theirs. We need it badly. We need them to retain their racial identities for us to distinguish ourselves.

Their racial identities reside in what they are. Ours is what we oppose. We're no more or less racist than other races and I've never known a person not to be racist, but we're proudly prejudiced against our forebears, each other, and ourselves. Our ideals define us, but they're the ideals of what we condemn.

The *Stuff White People Like* website pointed to the absurdity of our determination not to be racist, the falsity of it all. "*Since we are on the verge of...a black president*," wrote Kristen Warner the third Monday in January 2008, "*it seems important to explain why white people want black friends. Every white person wants a black friend like Barack: good-looking, well-spoken, and non-violent. Obviously, whites want black friends so as not to appear racist...However, if we dig deeper what we notice about white people is not if they have black friends but in fact, how many black friends they have. White people like numbers. They like to count things like stars in the sky and the death toll at Mt. Everest and the number of times they've seen Tori Amos and/or Phish in concert. Counting the number of black friends is then clearly a divine imperative. The number of black friends white people possess also illustrates their comfort with black culture. Here's a handy guide to the number system:*

"1 – The white novice. This black friend is the gateway to helping white people understand gang signs and Vietnamese beauty supply stores. This black friend is probably the only black friend for many white people and when they all hang out (because white people hang out) they bring their "mutual" black friend with them.

"2 – The white black club-goer. Two black friends serve as bodyguards when white people go to black clubs to see how exactly one "pops, drops and locks" it.

"3 – 4 – The white BET-er…" This presumably referred to Black Entertainment Television.

"5 and up – Impossible."

Our feelings around race have become a long litany of paradoxes we never resolve. Nor do we try; it's much too difficult. We find the best thing is not to consider them, but the only means of reconciling them is our relentless opposition to white people's racism. We think we like other races by not liking ourselves, love them by not loving ourselves, but we don't like or love them as much as we reject our past racism.

We choose when to feel our racial identities. We reject talk of race, but recognise race to feel obliged to help other races. We boast our social conscience when distant and passing strangers feel pain, but don't let our people's suffering interrupt our late-morning glory. We fail our obligations to others and dejectedly wallow in shame.

Our guilt is racial, pride is not. We accord collective guilt for the wrongdoings of our race damned forever, but never collective pride. We're not free to cherish the great things our race did and do.

For the goodness we do, we espouse the goodness of the human spirit. We give all the world credit for our kind deeds, steadfastly refusing to love ourselves.

Our wrongdoings are ours alone. While other races don't countenance they could do very much wrong, we don't countenance we could do very much right, except apologise and apologise again. We regret with unwavering humility, even crude arrogance, for being so remorseful.

Other race's wrongdoings blight the whole human species. We hate ourselves a little more.

Other race's kind deeds are theirs alone. We have reason to like them more.

We feel belonging not from our race but from being part of a mob: a vengeful, cruel mob. We shout down white racists because other people do, when saying anything else would be hard. Lambasting white racism lets us release contempt and even hatred within us, venting emotions we daren't otherwise vent. No one defends white racists, no one saves them. It's the easy assault, the coward's assault. All the tribal instincts other races express through their racial identities we express through our new-found opposition to white racism: our new Western tribalism.

Can we not feel for our race what people of other races feel for theirs? History is filled with conflicts between peoples, empires, and aspiring empires, of which Europeans were no more responsible than other races across Asia, Africa, the Americas, and the oceans. We explored the world, but didn't colonise countries with something like civilisation securely and peacefully in place, such as Siam and Tonga. They both became nation states with modern freedoms and laws in response to approaching European empires.

Racial and religious discrimination have been far more complex through history and remains far more complex than our present-day narratives suggest. Through the nineteenth century, continuing well after Negro slavery ended, signs and advertisements in America often expressly excluded Irish people from admission and jobs.

Black American abolitionist Frederick Douglass, a former slave, saw the plight of Irish in Ireland and also poor Irish in America protecting their menial jobs from black competition. *"Perhaps no class of our fellow-citizens has carried this prejudice against color to a point more extreme and dangerous than have our Catholic Irish fellow-citizens,"* he wrote in his 1846 autobiography *The Life and Times of Frederick Douglass, "and yet no people on the face of the earth have been more relentlessly persecuted and oppressed on account of race and religion, than have this same Irish people."*

Through the totality of British and American history, discrimination against Roman Catholic Irish exceeded discrimination against any other race. That might have been a reason that Roman Catholic Irish in America came to be at the forefront of opposing any form of discrimination by white people.

We can decide what our racial identity should mean, much as other races decide theirs for themselves. If we celebrated other races' values instead of other races, we'd consider the implications of them retaining racial loyalties not just in countries once ours but in countries still theirs. We'd imagine us identifying with our race as people of other races identify with theirs, if we can accommodate existential challenges to our anti-racial identity.

I'd rather another word, but the R-word carries too much misnomer from common usage for me to change it. We could speak of racialism to mean our recognition of race, consciousness of our equitable reality, of whatever depth and breadth is true. We could speak of loyalism to our wide racial kin, with the comfort of them being a little loyal back to us.

Soft breaths of racism require recognition of the reality of race; racism flows inevitably from race. We can enjoy racial identities without prejudice to others. We can honour our forebears as they sought to honour us, whatever they foolishly believed. Saying we're worthy of self-love, our forebears loved us more than we love ourselves, offering us self-affection we're stridently determined to deny. We can care about our people long after we're dead, trusting our descendants not to hate us for what we foolishly believe. Most profoundly of all, we can strive for our future as other races strive for theirs.

Weary as I am of the white man's burden, a gentle touch of racism can be looking after those of *our* race needing looking after. Ultimately everyone does.

When we care about people, we can care about our people too, without meaning others harm. Western social consciences could mean caring about European peoples suffering socially, politically, or economically: aiding our own without malice to others. When our people hurt, we can help them, instead of damning them for their paltry weak failings. We can consider their material comforts and human satisfaction, peace of mind and security walking the streets. All they might fear is being individuals left alone. One day, some from among them might help my family or me, but that's no reason to persevere.

Racism need only be fact, reason, and fairness applied to

matters of race. It need only be love and loyalty. If we have racial guilt, then so does every other race for its crimes, but we should also have racial pride for the good things we've done. All in all, I think we've done pretty well. We can feel the merits in what our kin achieved without denying our blunders. The sectarian murderers who kill passers-by in Ulster and Britain make me ashamed. Far more people than that make me proud: our heroes and heroines in wartime and peace.

Like intelligent and civilised Chinese in China, Japanese in Japan, and other races elsewhere, intelligent and civilised European peoples can be racist. We can enjoy our countries much as they enjoy theirs. Our forebears left our countries for us much as their forebears wanted their countries for them.

Racism needn't be derision of other races. Loving our race doesn't mean hating others, but we can't resume loving other races until we resume loving our own. We could leave other races to form and express their views about us, without us telling them to hate ours and without them deciding we should hate ours too. We could help them because we feel it's morally right, not because we feel obliged or ashamed; assessing potential expenditures with regard to what else we could do with our money and time. We should feel good when we are good.

It's not trivialising that most infamous of holocausts to say that we have at least as much reason as other races to enjoy self-respecting racism. Loving our race doesn't mean constructing concentration camps, any more than Japanese valuing theirs are preparing to set British servicemen on death marches or Mongols valuing theirs are massacring Hungarians. Loving ourselves doesn't make us Nazis.

The great travesties of the world aren't what we think our forebears did to others, but what we're now doing to ourselves: it need be our only shame. We're not alone in having harmed other peoples and our own, but no other race has helped more people than we've helped through history and are still helping. Nor is any other race crueller to its forebears or more wilfully neglectful of its own than we now are. Instead of ruefully regretting what is now the past, we'll come to rue what is now the present, through the late twentieth and early twenty-first centuries.

I am what I've always been, although it took me a while to realise as much. No government believes me, no law on earth recognises me, but I am Australian British just as my mother was. Without distraction by residency or rules of citizenship, I'm British: Australian or not. We're the people, my people, of whom we're a part: a people in whom we belong.

If I hated my race, preferring the company of other races, then nobody would mind. I don't. I like the presence of my people, seeing the goodness we've done instead of only the bad. If I wanted to advance other races at the expense of my own then we'd think that was wonderful, but I care deeply about our fortune and misfortune. I wish other races every happiness and success, but not at the expense of my own. In a world of finite resources, the smartest, most skilled, and hardest working people deserve more than others. They should have the right to earn and keep wealth for their families and race.

So should we. I want to help the sick, weak, and poor of my family and race. If I weren't white, descended from ancient European peoples, such sentiments would be fine, but I am.

Somewhere beyond shame and pride, we could simply appreciate being us. Unlike much of the rest of the world, our racial loyalties needn't abandon the interests of others. Our race's interests need only prevail, at least a little, above others. It's a strange feeling to realise I'm something I'd have once insisted I'm not, but for seeing European peoples as being peoples, real peoples, worthy of my affection, I'm one of those white people we look upon aghast. For respecting my race, I'm racist.

BIBLIOGRAPHY, REFERENCES

Articles

Alcindor, Yamiche with the *Associated Press* news service, 'Asian-American groups accuse Harvard of racial bias in admissions,' *USA Today* newspaper, 16 May 2015.

Barrett, Steve and Natalie O'Brien, 'Cronulla race riot response 'flawed',' *The Australian* newspaper, 20 October 2006.

Bignell, Paul, 'Uncovered: Churchill's warnings about the 'Hebrew bloodsuckers',' *The Independent* newspaper, 11 March 2007. A rebuttal was Richard Langworth, 'Churchill Accused of Anti-Semitism – Conclusion: Nonsense,' *Churchill Centre*. Antoine Capet, 'The Creeds of the Devil: Churchill between the Two Totalitarianisms, 1917-1945,' *Finest Hour Online*, 31 August 2009.

Bradsher, Keith with Hilda Wang, 'In China, an Instant Star and an Emerging Symbol,' *The New York Times* newspaper, 14 February 2012. Uncredited, 'Mayweather Slams 'Linsanity' On Twitter, Says Hype Due To Race,' *CBS New York* with *The Associated Press* news service, 14 February 2012. Mackenzie Weinger, 'Rep. Chu blasts ESPN Lin racial slur,' *Politico* news service, 20 February 2012. Uncredited, 'ESPN fires employee for offensive Jeremy Lin headline,' *Associated Press* news service published at *The Sydney Morning Herald* newspaper, 20 February 2012.

Buck, Tobias, 'Netanyahu's Holocaust rhetoric under fire,' *Financial Times* newspaper, 20 March 2012.

Burke, Kelly, 'Little Korea ready to rise from melting pot,' *The Sydney Morning Herald* newspaper, 26 May 2012.

Caldwell, Anna, 'Plan to change Punjab Place to Oak Tree Place in Logan,' *The Courier-Mail* newspaper, 13 August 2009. Tanveer Ahmed, 'Cultures dance in harmony in new land,' *The Sydney Morning Herald* newspaper, 19 January 2010. Maria Galinovic, 'Indian community elders are given a helping hand,' *St George and Sutherland Shire Leader*, 16 June 2013.

Carlton, Jeff, 'Riot police separate protesters in Texas town,' *Associated Press* news service published at *Breitbart News*, 21 July 2009.

Chong, Patty, '35 years on, I still fight racism,' *The Verdict* at *WA Today*, 24 July 2008. John Garnaut and Maya Li, 'China calls for a people's army to march on Canberra to defend torch,' *The*

Sydney Morning Herald newspaper, 16 April, 2008. Peter Cai, 'Ballerina's fancy footwork on China,' *The Age* newspaper, 16 July 2012, concerning the Miss Chinese Cosmos Australia pageant.

Curtin, Jennie, 'Note' on memorial irks Turks,' *The Sydney Morning Herald* newspaper, 13 August 2010. Sarah Sedghi, 'Armenians mark 100 years since Ottoman massacres; Vladimir Putin says no justification for mass murder,' *Australian Broadcasting Corporation* news, 24 April 2015.

Daily Mail Reporter, 'Tennis player Caroline Wozniacki accused of 'racist' impersonation of Serena Williams by stuffing bra and pants,' *Daily Mail* newspaper, 11 December 2012. Uncredited, 'Caroline Wozniacki sorry for making up kangaroo attack story,' *Agence France-Presse* news service published in *The Sydney Morning Herald* newspaper, 24 January 2011.

Devine, Miranda, 'The tragedy of sit-down money,' *The Daily Telegraph* newspaper, 2 April 2011.

Diamond, Laura, ''All we want to do is celebrate white identity' – White Student Union forms at Georgia State University,' *The New York Times* news service published at *The Sydney Morning Herald* newspaper, 1 August 2013.

Dillon, Anthony, 'Addressing disadvantage is no identity game,' *The Drum*, 3 November 2011.

Dominiczak, Peter, 'Labour MP embarrassed after claiming that 'white or black' smoke tweet about the Pope is about race,' *The Telegraph* newspaper, 13 March 2013.

Downes, Stephen, 'Trujillo latest victim of News Corp's racist toons writes,' *Crikey*, 27 February 2009. Ian Verrender, 'Adios, amigo, to the man who enfeebled Telstra,' *The Sydney Morning Herald* newspaper, 23 May 2009. Gabrielle Costa and others, 'Racist, backward: Sol's parting shot,' *The Sydney Morning Herald* newspaper, 26 May 2009. An *Australian Broadcasting Corporation News* report that evening included Trujillo referring to Australia's immigration policies having been relaxed only thirty years earlier. Adele Horin, 'Sol, your wake-up call is important: we've no good reason to be smug,' *The Sydney Morning Herald* newspaper, 30 May 2009.

Ehrenstein, David, 'Obama the 'Magic Negro',' *Los Angeles Times* newspaper, 7 March 2007. Josh Tyrangiel, 'Ocean's Thirteen, the Interview,' *Time* magazine, 30 May 2007, quoting Matt

Damon. Ann Sanner, 'Ferraro's Remarks About Obama Decried,' *Associated Press* news service, 11 March 2008. Jake Tapper, 'Kerry: Obama Could Help US Relations with Muslim Nations 'Because He's a Black Man',' in *Political Punch, Australian Broadcasting Corporation News*, 20 March 2008. Uncredited, 'Young voters: Obama's race as an asset, non-issue,' *China Daily* newspaper, 6 June 2008.

Elliott, Tim and others, 'Australian cricket 'needs ethnic stars',' *The Sydney Morning Herald* newspaper, 25 August 2009.

Espach, Alison, "Black Culture' Blamed for Hurricane Katrina Woes,' *Cybercast News Service*, 13 July 2006.

Feller, Ben, 'Obama sure Sotomayor would restate 2001 comment,' *Associated Press* news service published by *Yahoo! News*, 29 May 2009. Uncredited, 'The 'Empathy' Nominee: Is Sonia Sotomayor judicially superior to 'a white male'?' *The Wall Street Journal* newspaper, 27 May 2009. Patrick Hynes, 'Sotomayor Enters Confirmation Process with Miers-Like Numbers,' *Now! Hampshire*, 10 July 2009, with Cardinal Hayes '71 comments on 12 July 2009.

Field, Michael, 'NZ offers Samoa abject apology over colonial deaths,' *Agence France-Presse* news service, Mulinu'u, Samoa, 3 June 2002.

Fitzgerald, Joe, 'Lott's offhand remark not worth demand for his head,' *The Boston Herald* newspaper, 18 December 2002, quoting John Kerry.

Flock, Elizabeth, 'HUD Proposes Plan to Racially, Economically Integrate Neighborhoods,' *US News*, 9 August 2013. Paul Sperry, 'Obama collecting personal data for a secret race database,' *New York Post* newspaper, 18 July 2015.

Fried, Rebecca, 'No Irish Need Deny: Evidence for the Historicity of NINA Restrictions in Advertisements and Signs,' *Journal of Social History* (2015), 4 July 2015. Thom Dunn, 'A 14-year-old girl disproves a college professor's published theory on racism...by Googling it,' *Upworthy*, 14 August 2015.

Garnaut, John with Leesha McKenny, 'Australian businesswoman falls foul of China's legal system,' *The Sydney Morning Herald* newspaper, 23 August 2011. Peter Cai and Barry FitzGerald, 'Fears Beijing targeting ethnic Chinese executives,' *The Sydney Morning Herald* newspaper, 26 December 2011. Philip Wen, 'Jailed executives are Chinese, Carr told,' *The Sydney Morning*

Herald newspaper, 15 May 2012.

Gibbs, Stephen, 'Harrison has run his race,' *The Sydney Morning Herald* newspaper, 26 March 2005, concerning Todd Curley and David Cockatoo-Collins. Will Brodie, 'Racist comments cost Pie fan his membership,' *The Age* newspaper, 5 June 2012.

Gibson, Richard, 'Lehmann banned for five one-day internationals,' *The Independent* newspaper, 18 January 2003.

Goodwin, M, 'Sarah Palin is taking a bigger beating because she's a Republican woman,' *The New York Times* newspaper, 5 October 2008, quoting the American who complained that George W Bush "never thought about race."

Grace, Robyn, 'NT tourism accused of using racist term in Google ad,' *The Age* newspaper, 11 May 2010. Andi Mastrosavas, "Abo' is not just an abbreviation of 'Aboriginal',' *The Punch*, 20 July 2011.

Griffin, Michelle, 'Rangaism isn't racism,' *The Sydney Morning Herald* newspaper, 20 September 2010.

Guyer, Julian, 'Australian golfer Steve Elkington in Twitter 'Pakki' racism row,' *Agence France-Presse* news service published at *Australian Golf Digest* and the *News Limited Network*, 28 July 2013.

Haines, Errin, 'Couple's 'buy black' experiment becomes a movement,' *Associated Press* news service, Atlanta, 12 May 2009.

Halper, Daniel, 'Obama: 'Be Confident in Your Heritage. Be Confident in Your Blackness,' *The Weekly Standard* newspaper, 7 May 2016.

Harnden, Toby, 'Black Republicans offer hope after Barack Obama's failures on race,' *The Telegraph* newspaper, 9 October 2010.

Hastings, Chris, 'Quangos blackball... oops, sorry... veto 'racist' everyday phrases,' *The Sunday Times* newspaper, 23 August 2009.

Hernandez, Daisy, 'Across America, Latino Community Sighs with Relief,' *National Public Radio*, 12 January 2011.

Hoe Yeen Nie, 'Singaporeans of mixed race allowed to 'double barrel' race in IC,' *Channel News Asia*, 12 January 2010. Nathan Klein, 'Singapore party ban on whites at Botanic Gardens event attacked as racist,' *The Daily Telegraph* newspaper, 15 October 2013.

Horan, Patrick, 'Kevin Sheedy cops verbal hammering from soccer pundit Craig Foster after post-match 'immigration' comments,' *Australian Associated Press* news service published on the *News*

Limited Network, 13 May 2013.

Horin, Adele, 'Youth call Australia home, but cling to heritage,' *The Sydney Morning Herald* newspaper, 6 November 2010. *The Australian* newspaper, 25 February 2011 credited the article to Horin.

Hunter, Melanie, 'Biden: '11 Million Undocumented Aliens Are Already Americans in My View',' *Cybercast News Service*, 27 March 2014. Uncredited, 'Obama: Being American is 'not a matter of blood or birth',' *The New York Post* newspaper, 1 July 2011.

Jackson, Glenn and Michael Lallo, 'Morrow's sorrow over joke 'misinterpreted as racist',' *The Sydney Morning Herald* newspaper, 9 May 2013.

Jones, Susan, 'U.N.-Backed Summit Seeks 'Social Justice' for African Descendants,' *Cybercast News Service*, 27 May 2011.

Jopson, Debra, 'Black heart of Redfern doesn't miss a beat,' *The Sydney Morning Herald* newspaper, 10 July 2009.

Kaiser, Shannon, '25 Things Happy People Do Differently,' *Mind Body Green*, 1 August 2013.

Khumalo, Sibongile, 'World celebrates as South Africa's Mandela turns 91,' *The Sydney Morning Herald* newspaper, 18 July 2009. Uncredited, 'Mandela joins stars at London gig,' *BBC News*, 28 June 2008.

Knox, Malcolm, 'Context the key when punishing racial vilification,' *Crikey* daily mail, 13 October 2010. David Beniuk, 'Parramatta's Timana Tahu to play for New Zealand Maori after missing Four Nations selection,' *Australian Associated Press* news service published at *Fox News*, 8 October 2010. James Hooper, 'Timana Tahu laughs off suggestion he racially vilified Aboriginal youth during Koori Knockout,' *The Daily Telegraph* newspaper, 8 October 2010.

Lambert, Angela, 'Talking pictures with Annie Leibovitz,' *The Independent* newspaper, 3 March 1994.

Laws, Mike, 'Why we capitalize 'Black' (and not 'white'),' *Columbia Journalism Review*, 16 June 2020.

Le Grand, Chip, 'Suicide policeman faced sack over offensive emails, Simon Overland confirms,' *The Australian* newspaper, 25 March 2010. Gallagher, Ian and Christine Challand, 'Lab technician kills himself after complaint over his joke that black friend 'should hide from immigration officers',' *The Mail on*

Sunday newspaper, 11 April 2010. Niger-man of Nigeria's response was posted on the *News Limited Network* at 11.04pm on 11 April 2010. Mark Hodge and Ian Murphy, "AN ABSOLUTE TRAGEDY': Schoolgirl hanged herself over fears of online backlash over racially offensive Instagram snap,' *The Sun* newspaper, 28 August 2016.

Lentini, Rosemarie and Edith Bevin, 'Surnames reflect changing suburbia,' *The Daily Telegraph* newspaper, 9 September 2010. Adele Horin, 'Lost inside our cultural ghettos,' *The Sydney Morning Herald* newspaper, 30 October 2010. Andrew Jakubowicz, 'Is Sydney a city of enclaves?' *The Sydney Morning Herald* newspaper, 12 November 2011.

Lott, Maxim, 'Calling America 'Land of Opportunity' offensive, University of California warns professors,' *Fox News*, 15 June 2015.

Lowe, Adrian, 'British Airways embarrassed over racist retweet,' *The Sydney Morning Herald* newspaper, 19 November 2012.

Lulay, Stephanie, 'New Anti-Gentrification Signs Demand, 'White People Out of Pilsen',' *DNA Info*, 26 October 2015.

Lyall, Sarah, 'Britain Seeks Its Essence, and Finds Punch Lines,' *The New York Times* newspaper, 26 January 2008.

Maiden, Samantha, 'I'm offering you nothing – Julia Gillard's response to dumped senator Trish Crossin,' *The Daily Telegraph* newspaper, 7 February 2013. Christopher Walsh, 'Senator Nova Peris sought taxpayers' money to help her to carry out a 'freaky' extra-marital sexual tryst with Olympic medallist Ato Boldon,' *NT News*, 29 October 2014.

Mann, Simon, 'Tea Party rally stirs bitter resentment from rights groups,' *The Sydney Morning Herald* newspaper, 28 August 2010. Christopher Hitchens, 'Fighting Words – White Fright,' *Slate* magazine, 30 August 2010.

Mark, David, 'AFL's position on Indigenous history of Aussie Rules leaves game's historians baffled,' *ABC News*, 14 June 2019.

Martinez, Ana Isabel and others, 'Chavez offers talks with 'black man' in W. House,' *Reuters* news service, 2 November 2008. Uncredited, 'Obama 'a major step' for humanity: Canada governor general,' *Agence France-Presse* news service, 18 January 2009. Staff, 'Samuel L. Jackson: I Voted for Obama BECAUSE HE'S BLACK,' *Thirty Mile Zone*, 11 February 2012, quoting

Ebony magazine, March 2012.

McGuinness, Damien, 'Lithuanian blonde island plan raises eyebrows,' *BBC News Riga*, 2 October 2010.

McKay, Hollie, 'Angie Harmon: I'm Not Racist Because I Disagree With Obama,' *Fox News*, 30 March 2009. Christian Toto, 'For political comedians, the joke's not on Obama,' *The Washington Times* newspaper, 5 May 2009. Paul Bond, 'Ed Asner Explains Hollywood Silence on Obama, Syria: They 'Don't Want to Feel Anti-Black',' *Hollywood Reporter*, 6 September 2013.

Mellman, Mark and Michael Bloomfield, 'Israel and the Jewish vote,' *The Jerusalem Post* newspaper, 12 November 2008.

Michael, Ali, 'I Sometimes Don't Want to Be White Either,' *Huffington Post Black Voices*, 16 June 2015. Aurelius Pundit, 'HuffPo Writer: I Will Not Have Children So I Will not Spread my White Privilege,' *The Social Memo*, 19 June 2015.

Miranda, Charles, 'British plan ANZAC whitewash,' *News Limited Network*, 9 January 2014.

Mitchell, Peter, 'White Aussie woman sparks racial fury – by winning job at black magazine,' *The Daily Telegraph* newspaper, 3 August 2010.

Molitorisz, Sacha, 'Tribes of the Sydney,' *The Sydney Morning Herald* newspaper, 7 January 2010.

Moore, Malcolm, 'Martin Luther King memorial made in China,' *The Telegraph* newspaper, 22 August 2011.

Morrissey, Tracie Egan, 'Racist Teens Forced to Answer for Tweets About the 'Nigger' President,' *Jezebel*, 9 November 2012. Kashmir Hill, 'Should Teenagers Have Racist Election Tweets in their Google Results for Life? Jezebel Votes Yes,' *Forbes* magazine, 9 November 2012.

Munro, Peter, 'Why so few spoke up for a woman who was abused on a city bus,' *The Age* newspaper, 22 November 2012. Joe Hildebrand, 'We should make an example of dumb racists,' *The Punch*, 21 November 2012. David Penberthy, 'A nation of uncouth bastards,' *The Punch*, 25 November 2012.

Olshansky, Jay and others, 'Differences In Life Expectancy Due To Race And Educational Differences Are Widening, And Many May Not Catch Up,' *Health Affairs*, Volume 31 Number 8, August 2012. Sabrina Tavernise, 'Reversing Trend, Life Span Shrinks for Some Whites,' *The New York Times* newspaper, 20 September 2012, citing David Cutler in *Health Affairs* in 2008.

Hope Yen, 'Exclusive: Signs of Declining Economic Security,' *Associated Press* news service, 29 July 2013, quoting the numbers of black and white people in poverty and household poverty by the mother's race.

Pierik, Jon, 'Schoolgirl apologises to 'heartbroken' Swans star,' *The Sydney Morning Herald* newspaper, 25 May 2013. Mark Macgugan, 'Pies apologise to Goodes after alleged racial slur,' *AFL Network*, 24 May 2013. Adrian Crawford, 'Adam Goodes 'gutted' by racial slur but wants AFL fan educated,' *Australian Broadcasting Corporation News*, 25 May 2013. Stathi Paxinos, 'McGuire apologises for Goodes King Kong gaffe,' *The Sydney Morning Herald* newspaper, 29 May 2013. Anthony Sharwood, 'It would be a good thing for everyone if we heard less of Eddie McGuire,' *The Punch*, 29 May 2013. Andrew Bolt, 'End this disgrace and get on with the game of footy,' *Herald Sun* newspaper, 29 May 2013. The first Australian news report of the Sweden riots I saw was through *Australian Broadcasting Corporation News* late on 26 May 2013.

Pilger, John, 'The Friends of Pol Pot,' *The Nation* magazine, 11 May 1998.

Protzman, Ferdinand, 'Upheaval In The East; The East Germans Issue An Apology For Nazis' Crimes,' *The New York Times* newspaper, 13 April 1990. Nicholas Kulish, 'Honoring Nazi victims as witnesses fade,' *International Herald Tribune* newspaper, 28 January 2008. Uncredited, 'Germans refuse to forget Nazi past,' *The Telegraph* newspaper, 31 January 2008. Anthony Faiola with Ruth Eglash, "Pudding Man' who left Israel for Germany reveals his identity,' *Washington Post* newspaper, 17 October 2014.

Quinn, Karl, "Racially insensitive' computer game faces challenge over title,' *The Age* newspaper, 2 September 2013. Daniel Tran, 'Time to ditch monarch, says republican activist,' *Monash Weekly*, 10 December 2012.

Ralston, Nick, "Mao's last dancer' named top Aussie dad,' *The Sydney Morning Herald* newspaper, 28 August 2009.

Robinson, Jennifer, 'The hero too many of us still don't know,' *The Sydney Morning Herald* newspaper, 14 August 2012, concerning Peter Norman.

Rush, James, 'Goldsmiths University diversity officer explains she cannot be racist or sexist to white men because she is an ethnic minority woman,' *The Independent* newspaper, 12 May 2015. Gaz Jeffries, 'Goldsmiths diversity officer criticised for 'kill all white men' tweets,' *Pink News*, 20 May 2015.

Semple, Kirk with others, '8 Facing Charges in Wake of Death of a Fellow G.I.,' *The New York Times* newspaper, 21 December 2011, concerning Danny Chen.

Seper, Jerry, 'Panel finds Justice reluctant to take cases of white victims,' *The Washington Times* newspaper, 6 December 2010.

Sheehan, Paul, 'Rudd's electoral cracks about to open further,' *The Sydney Morning Herald* newspaper, 9 June 2010, concerning the *Bringing Them Home* report of 1997 that accused the Australian people of committing genocide against the Aborigines.

Smith, Patrick, *The Australian* newspaper, 14 February 2003, which soon disappeared from the website but was cited in Habib's entry at the *Daily*, 14 February 2003.

Somerville, Ewan, 'Sheffield SU bans white students from attending 'anti-racism' meetings,' *The Sheffield Tab* at *The Tab*, 8 October 2019. Darren Burke, 'Students at the University of Sheffield are to be paid to challenge language on campus which could be seen as racist,' *Sheffield Telegraph*, 14 January 2020.

Stewart, Matt, 'Racing officials defend decision to rename filly Blackman,' *Herald Sun* newspaper, 20 July 2012.

Symons, Emma-Kate, 'Colonial past continues to haunt France,' *The Australian* newspaper, 9 January 2010. Uncredited, 'Sarkozy tells nation leaving euro would be 'madness',' *Agence France-Presse* news service, 31 December 2010. Peter Malcolm, 'Video Shows French Muslims Undisturbed by Charlie Hebdo and Supermarket Attacks,' *Ben Shapiro's Truth Revolt*, 17 February 2015.

Tapper, Jake, 'Obama Talks More About 'Typical White Person' Grandmother,' *Political Punch* in *Australian Broadcasting Corporation News*, 20 March 2008.

Uncredited, 'Ashes: ABC employee announcing at England tour match removed for racially insensitive behaviour towards Monty Panesar,' *Australian Broadcasting Corporation News*, 30 November 2013. Uncredited, 'Ashes: ABC ground announcer denies making racial slur against Monty Panesar in England tour match,' *Australian Broadcasting Corporation News*, 2 December 2013.

Uncredited, 'Australia still racist, says surgeon Charlie Teo,'

Australian Broadcasting Corporation News, 19 January 2012.

Uncredited, 'Barry: 'We've got to do something about these Asians coming in',' *The Washington Examiner* newspaper, 5 April 2012.

Uncredited, 'Beijing restaurant sign banning Vietnamese, Filipinos and dogs triggers online fury,' *Agence France-Presse* news service published at *News Limited Network*, 28 February 2013.

Uncredited, 'City Council Warns 'Crack Ho' Comments 'Intolerable', Calls For Diversity In Talk Radio,' *CBS Los Angeles News*, 21 March 2012.

Uncredited, 'Livingstone breaks down in tears at slave trade memorial,' *Daily Mail* newspaper, 24 August 2007. Uncredited, 'British woman convicted of slavery,' *Agence France-Presse* news service published at *News Limited Network*, 17 March 2011, concerning Saeeda Khan.

Uncredited, 'Matrix actor felt racist 'vibe',' *The Age* newspaper, 5 May 2003, concerning Laurence Fishburne.

Uncredited, 'Norway offers its first Holocaust apology,' *Reuters* news service published at the *Jerusalem Post* newspaper, 27 January 2012.

Uncredited, 'Tony Abbott says Australians should learn about British history,' *Australian Associated Press* news service, 13 October 2008. Simon of Sydney, Jeepers of Brisbane, Robert Rowan of Adelaide, and aka of Sydney commented in response to the article at *News Limited Network*.

Uncredited, 'Union official flees Singapore for Perth after tired, racial rant' introduced as 'Aussie flees Singapore after racist Facebook rant,' *News Limited Network*, 11 October 2012, concerning Amy Cheong.

Uncredited, 'Vote for the black guy,' Port Adelaide council election posters urge,' *Australian Broadcasting Corporation News*, 15 October 2014.

Various, *Ignatian* magazine, December 2011, especially page 11.

Veronese, Keith, 'During World War II, Japan plotted to unleash a plague on the United States,' *io9*, 10 May 2012. Cameron Stewart, 'Defence told PM Kevin Rudd to stay silent on Centaur to keep onside with Japan,' *The Australian* newspaper, 21 January 2010. Uncredited, 'Mitsubishi apologises for using US prisoners of war as slave labourers during World War II,' *Agence France-Presse* and *Reuters* news services published at *Australian Broadcasting Corporation News*, 20 July 2015.

Vigdor, Neil, 'Democrats drop Thomas Jefferson and Andrew Jackson names from annual fundraising dinner,' *Connecticut Post* newspaper, 23 July 2015.

Wells, Jamelle and others, 'Scouts feared paedophile Steven Larkins would use 'race card' if sacked, royal commission told,' *Australian Broadcasting Corporation News*, 17 September 2013.

West, Lindy, 'Hilarious Crazy Lady Commandeers Sweden's Twitter Feed, Has Questions about Jews,' *Jezebel*, 14 Jun 2012.

Whitbourn, Michaela, 'SBS presenter Scott McIntyre sacked over 'inappropriate' Anzac Day tweets,' *The Sydney Morning Herald* newspaper, 26 April 2015.

Whyte, Sarah and Daniel Lewis, 'Was this uni Raj night racist?' *The Sydney Morning Herald* newspaper, 10 June 2012.

Williams, George, 'Race vote should offer protection all round,' *The Sydney Morning Herald* newspaper, 27 September 2011.

Williams, Patricia, 'Is Anti-White Bias a Problem?' *The New York Times* newspaper, 23 May 2011.

Winslow, Olivia, 'Census report sees minorities becoming majority by 2042,' *Newsday*, 13 August 2008.

Woodberry, Robert, 'The Missionary Roots of Liberal Democracy,' *American Political Science Review*, Volume 106 Number 2, May 2012. Natasha Moore and Robert Woodberry, 'Counterintuitive Colonialism,' *Centre for Public Christianity*, 30 August 2015.

Books

Baden-Powell, Robert, 1857-1941, *The Downfall of Prempeh: A Diary of Life with the Native Levy in Ashanti* (1896). See Raheem Kassam, 'Baden-Powell, Whose Statue the Left Tried to Remove, Led the Anti-Slavery Force in Africa Where Kings in Kente Cloth Sold Slaves for Human Sacrifice,' *The National Pulse*, 13 June 2020.

Churchill, Ward, born 1947, *A Little Matter of Genocide* (1997).

Churchill, Ward, born 1947, *Kill the Indian, Save the Man: The Genocidal Impact of American Indian Residential Schools* (2004).

CIA World Factbook listed the richest countries on earth per capita.

Courtenay, Bryce, 1933-2012, *The Power Of One* (1989).

Davis, David Brion, *Inhuman Bondage: The Rise and Fall of Slavery in the New World* (2006), Oxford University Press, US, especially page 82, referring to North African slave traders.

Deane, William, born 1931, *Directions: A Vision For Australia* (2002), summarised at 'Our history, not rewritten but put right,' *The Sydney Morning Herald* newspaper, 25 November 2002.

Douglass, Frederick, circa 1818-1895, *The Life and Times of Frederick Douglass* (1846). Tom Chaffin, *Giant's Causeway: Frederick Douglass's Irish Odyssey and the Making of an American Visionary* (2014). Joan Walsh. 'Frederick Douglass' Irish sojourn: A bracing look at his encounters with poverty and prejudice across the Atlantic,' *Salon*, 30 December 2014.

Groseclose, Tim, *Cheating: An Insider's Report on the Use of Race in Admissions at UCLA* (2014). Maxim Lott, 'UCLA prof says stats prove school's admissions illegally favor blacks,' *Fox News*, 13 May 2014.

Hanfstaengl, Ernst, with Brian Connell, *Hitler: The Missing Years*, 1957. Antoine Capet, 'The Creeds of the Devil: Churchill between the Two Totalitarianisms, 1917-1945,' *Finest Hour Online*, 31 August 2009.

Helms, Janet, *A Race is a Nice Thing to Have: A Guide to Being a White Person or Understanding the White Persons in Your Life* (1992), Content Communications. Janet Helms, 'Toward a Model of White Racial Identity Development,' in *Black and White Racial Identity: Theory, Research and Practice* (1990), Greenwood Press, especially page 50. Jennifer Wozab, 'Helm's Model of White Identity Development,' Exploring College Student Development Theory, University of Utah, 8 November 2010.

Hoffman, Michael, 1944-1990, *They Were White and They Were Slaves: The Untold History of the Enslavement of Whites in Early America* (1991).

Jordan, Don and Michael Walsh, *White Cargo: The Forgotten History of Britain's White Slaves in America* (2008), New York University Press. Joyce Hor-Chung Lau, *International Herald Tribune* newspaper, 28 April 2008. Gjohnsit, 'The slaves that time forgot,' *Daily Kos*, 27 December 2013. Sean O'Callaghan, *To Hell or Barbados: The Ethnic Cleansing of Ireland* (2000). Liam Hogan, 'The Myth of 'Irish Slaves' in the Colonies,' *Academia*, rejected any characterisation of them as slaves as being politically motivated, although his motivations appear politically motivated.

Keneally, Thomas, born 1935, *Australians: Eureka to the Diggers* (2011).

Lee, Harper, born 1926, *To Kill a Mockingbird*, (1960). Michelle Pauli, 'Harper Lee tops librarians' must-read list,' *The Guardian* newspaper, 2 March 2006.

Milton, Giles, *White Gold: The Extraordinary Story of Thomas Pellow and North Africa's One Million European Slaves* (2005) Hodder & Stoughton. Dan Neill, *Guardian* newspaper, June 27, 2004 and Ben-Peter Terpstra, *On Line Opinion*, 26 October 2004. Robert Davis, *Christian Slaves, Muslim Masters: White Slavery in the Mediterranean, the Barbary Coast and Italy, 1500–1800*, Palgrave Macmillan.

Morrison, Toni, born 1931, *A Mercy* (2008). Ben Naparstek, 'Mercy in a time of slavery,' *The Sydney Morning Herald* newspaper, 22 November 2008.

Morrison, Toni, born 1931, *Beloved* (1987). Andrea Sachs, '10 Questions for Toni Morrison,' *Time* magazine, 7 May 2008.

Perry, Imani, born 1972, *More Beautiful and More Terrible* (2011), New York University Press. Joel Gehrke, 'Schultz says 'break' is a 'southern racist term',' *The Examiner* (Washington) newspaper, 14 October 2011 ascribed the concept of post-intentional racism to Michael Eric Dyson speaking on the *Ed Schultz Show*, MSNBC.

Person-Lynn, Kwaku, *African Involvement in Atlantic Slave Trade*.

Safa, Reza, a Muslim who converted to Christianity, *Inside Islam: Exposing and Reaching the World of Islam*, 1997. Mark Silverberg, 'The Wahhabi Invasion of America,' 27 February 2003, cited official Saudi information concerning overseas expenditure by Saudi Arabia since 1973.

Seagrave, Sterling and Peggy Seagrave, *Gold Warriors: America's Secret Recovery of Yamashita's Gold* (2003), Verso. Chalmers Johnson, 'The Looting of Asia,' *London Review of Books*, Volume 25 Number 22, 20 November 2003.

von Clausewitz, Carl, 1780-1831, *On War* (1832), published posthumously by his wife. Thank God for the wives.

West, Cornel, born 1953, *Malcolm X and Black Rage* (1993), Race Matters, Beacon Press, especially pages 95 to 105.

Windschuttle, Keith, born 1942, *The Fabrication of Aboriginal History* (2002). Theodore Dalrymple, 'Why our intellectuals want to believe in genocide,' *New English Review*, published in *The Australian* newspaper, 6 July 2007. Mark Colvin interviewed Windschuttle on the *PM* radio programme, Australian

Broadcasting Corporation, broadcast on 12 December 2002.
Wouk, Herman, born 1915, *The Caine Mutiny* (1952).

Films

American Werewolf in London, An (1981), directed by John Landis, born 1950.

Battle on Shangganling Mountain (1956, China), with the theme song 'My Motherland' (1956). Matthew Robertson, 'US humiliated in eyes of Chinese by song used to inspire anti-Americanism,' *Epoch Times*, 22 January 2011.

Big Lift, The (1950), written by George Seaton. Paul Douglas played Henry "Hank" Kowalski. Bruni Löbel played Gerda. Charlotte Chandler, *Hello, I Must Be Going: Groucho and His Friends*, concerning George Seaton.

Bitter Springs (1950). Henry Murdock played Blackjack. Michael Pate played the trooper. Chips Rafferty played Wally King. The trooper's words I quote were made 25 minutes into the film.

Blazing Saddles (1974), written by Mel Brooks (born Melvin Kaminsky) and others, directed by Mel Brooks. Cleavon Little played Sheriff Bart. Gene Wilder played Jim, "The Waco Kid." Madeline Kahn played Lili von Shtüpp, "The Teutonic Titwillow."

Blues Brothers, The (1980), directed by John Landis and written by John Landis and Dan Aykroyd.

Bob & Carol & Ted & Alice (1969), written by Paul Mazurksy. Stephen Farber, 'A Night in Hollywood, a Day in Ukraine,' *The New York Times* newspaper, 31 December 2006.

Borat: Cultural Learnings of America for Make Benefit Glorious Nation of Kazakhstan (2006). Kirk Honeycutt's review of *Bruno* (2009), *Hollywood Reporter*, 26 June 2009.

Braveheart (1995) starring and directed by Mel Gibson. Joe Hildebrand, 'Mel Gibson: Cute, Crazy, Catholic,' *The Daily Telegraph* newspaper, 11 May 2009.

Chinese Zodiac (2012). Vivienne Chow, 'Jackie Chan back in action, branding US more corrupt than China,' *South China Morning Post* newspaper, 12 January 2013.

Django Unchained (2012) starring Jamie Foxx. Erika Parker, 'VIBE Cover Story: Django Unchained,' *Vibe* magazine, 28 November 2012. J J Anisiob, "As a black person it's always racial',' *Daily*

Mail newspaper, 14 December 2012.

Duck Soup (1933), starring Groucho Marx and three of his brothers.

Fortune Cookie, The (1966). Jack Lemmon played Harry Hinkle. Ron Rich played Luther "Boom Boom" Jackson. Cliff Osmond played Chester Purkey.

Heroes (1977), starring Henry Winkler.

High Anxiety (1978), written by Mel Brooks (born Melvin Kaminsky) and others, directed by Mel Brooks.

Hotel Rwanda (2004), written by Irishman Terry George, born 1952, and American Keir Pearson, born 1966.

Indiana Jones and the Last Crusade (1989).

Indiana Jones and the Temple of Doom (1984).

Lincoln (2012), based upon Doris Kearns Goodwin, *Team of Rivals: The Political Genius of Abraham Lincoln* (2005).

Magnificent Seven, The (1960), starring Yul Brynner and Steve McQueen, from an original script by Walter Newman, 1916-1993, revised by William Roberts, 1913-1997.

Naked Kiss, The (1964), written and directed by Samuel Fuller, 1912-1997.

Producers, The (1968), featuring the song 'Springtime for Hitler' (1968).

Raiders of the Lost Ark (1981), written by Lawrence Kasdan, born 1949, and directed by Steven Spielberg, born 1946.

Ring, The (1927), directed by Alfred Hitchcock. It used the word "*nigger*" in a caption after 44 minutes, 25 seconds.

Sapphires, The (2012). Karl Quinn, 'Furore over 'sexist, racist' Sapphires DVD cover for US release,' *The Sydney Morning Herald* newspaper, 2 August 2013.

Seekers, The (1954). *Internet Movie Database* reviews by David Atfield from Canberra on 1 September 1999 and Peter CMD from New Zealand on 4 August 2009.

Shawshank Redemption, The (1994).

Town Like Alice, A (1956).

Sunset Boulevard (1950).

When Harry Met Sally... (1989), written by Nora Ephron. Aire Kaplan, 'How Jews Revolutionised Comedy in America,' from a panel discussion at Skirball Cultural Centre, Los Angeles, published 22 August 2002.

Why Did I Get Married? (2007). Sean O'Sullivan, 'Delaware Supreme Court overturns cinema ruling,' *The News Journal*, 23 February

2011.

Judgments

Ricci v DeStefano 557 U.S. 557 (2009).

Nursery Rhymes

'Baa Baa Black Sheep'. Staff writers, "'Racist' Baa Baa Black Sheep put out to pasture,' *The Sunday Mail* (Queensland) newspaper, 27 February 2011.

'Humpty Dumpty'. Staff writers, "'Racist' Baa Baa Black Sheep put out to pasture,' *The Sunday Mail* (Queensland) newspaper, 27 February 2011.

Poems

Kipling, Rudyard, 1865-1936, 'The White Man's Burden' (1899), 12th edition of *McClure's* magazine. William Easterly, *The White Man's Burden: Why the West's Efforts to Aid the Rest Have Done So Much Ill and So Little Good* (2006), Penguin. Tom Peters, *The Little Big Things* (2011). Vaughn Aubuchon, 'Vaughn's one-page summaries,' *General Knowledge Reference*, detailed American foreign aid. Douglas Casey, 'Opportunity in Mozambique,' *Escape From America* magazine, 1996.

Reports

Villanger, Espen, 'Arab Foreign Aid: Disbursement Patterns, Aid Policies and Motives,' Chr. Michelsen Institute, CMI Report R 2007: 2, 2007.

Songs

'I Dream A Dream' (1980), music by Claude-Michel Schönberg, born 1944, and English lyrics by Herbert Kretzmer, born 1925, from a French libretto by Alain Boublil, born 1941, from the musical *Les Miserables* (1980).

'You've Got to Be Carefully Taught' (1949), from the musical *South Pacific* (1949, and a 1958 film), music by Richard Rodgers, 1902-

1979, lyrics by Oscar Hammerstein II, 1895-1960. Andrea Most, 'You've Got to Be Carefully Taught: The Politics of Race in Rodgers and Hammerstein's South Pacific,' *Theatre Journal*, Volume 52 Number 3, October 2000.

Television Programmes

All in the Family (1971-1979).

Animal Practice (2012 onwards). Daily Mail Reporter, 'NBC forced to apologise after ill-timed ad features a monkey doing gymnastics – right after showing Gabby Douglas' gold medal victory,' *Daily Mail* newspaper, 3 August 2012.

Black in America (2008-2012), Cable News Network. Paul Bedard, 'Soledad O'Brien: 'OK, white person, this is a conversation you clearly are uncomfortable with',' *The Washington Examiner* newspaper, 13 May 2013.

Empire (2012), British Broadcasting Corporation and Open University. Episode 5 'Doing Good' referred to David Livingstone.

Fashion Police (2010 onwards), E! Entertainment Television, February 2013. Uncredited, 'Joan Rivers not sorry for Heidi Klum Holocaust gag,' *News Limited Network*, 1 March 2013.

Get Smart (1965-1970), created by Mel Brooks (born Melvin Kaminsky) and Buck Henry (born Henry Zuckerman).

Good News Week (1996-2000, 2008-2012).

Happy Days (1974-1984), notably the episodes 'The Best Man' (1974) and 'Fonzie's new Friend' (1975).

Hogan's Heroes (1965-1971). Leslie Campbell Rampey, 'Hogan's Heroes and the Holocaust: The Association That Just Won't Go Away,' 14 April 2000.

Knowing Me, Knowing You, with Alan Partridge (1994-1995), starring Steve Coogan.

Midsomer Murders (1997 onwards), based on books by Caroline Graham. Uncredited, 'Creator defends all-white Midsomer,' *The Sydney Morning Herald* newspaper, 15 March 2011. Uncredited, 'Midsomer co-creator suspended over racial remarks,' *Agence France-Presse* news service published in *The Sydney Morning Herald* newspaper, 15 March 2011.

Mork & Mindy (1978-1982), notably the episode 'The Night They Raided Mind-ski's' (1980).

Newshour With Jim Lehrer, The (1995 onwards), PBS Television. The Bev Smith interview was in July 2009.

Portrait of a City: Paris (2010), referred to the flame above France's Tomb of the Unknown Soldier burning each night throughout the German occupation.

Skippy the Bush Kangaroo (1966-1970).

Till Death Us Do Part (1965-1975). Jay Richardson, 'Speak softly, carry a BIG SCHTICK: Is British TV ready for Jewish comedy?' *The Scotsman* newspaper, 19 April 2012 mentioned Johnny Speight was Jewish.

Tonight Show with Jay Leno, The (1992 onwards, especially 8 February 2013), NBC. Noel Sheppard, 'Leno on Snowstorm Nemo: 'Massachusetts Is Now Whiter than a Romney Family Reunion',' *Newsbusters*, 9 February 2013. John Ensslin, 'Obama quip stuns Citizen of the West banquet crowd,' *Rocky Mountain News*, 17 January 2008.

Top Gear (2002 onwards). Steve Coogan, 'Top Gear's offensive stereotyping has gone too far,' *The Guardian* newspaper, 5 February 2011. Adam Lusher, 'Jeremy Clarkson claims airport delays could be solved with 'a bit of racism',' *The Telegraph* newspaper, 5 May 2012.

Twilight Zone, The (1959-1964). Rod Serling wrote the episode 'He's Alive' (1963).

Uncensored (1998), Australian Broadcasting Corporation, with Jana Wendt. *Media Watch* (1989 onwards).

Vicar of Dibley, The (1994-2007). Uncredited, 'Soapie *Neighbours* slammed for being 'too white',' *The Sydney Morning Herald* newspaper, 18 July 2008.

World at War, The (1973).

ABOUT THE AUTHOR

Simon Lennon has travelled throughout Europe, America, Australasia, Asia, and the South Pacific, seeing how similar European peoples are to each other (wherever we live) and how different we of the West are to everyone else. He has university bachelor's degrees in science and law and university master's degrees in commerce and business. He is married with six children.

His non-fiction collection *The West* comprises the following sixteen books:

Mending the West
The Unnatural West: An Overview
The Tribeless West: An Overview
The Homeless West: An Overview
The Vanishing West: An Overview

Individualism
Western Individualism
The End of Natural Selection
The Need for Nations

Identity
People's Identity: Race and Racism
Of Whom We're Born: Race and Family
Biological Us: Gender and Sexuality

Nationalism
A Land to Belong: Nationalism
The Failure of Multiculturalism

Cultures
Reclaiming Western Cultures
Christendom Lost
Aiding Islam

He is also the author of another non-fiction book, two collections of short stories, and five novels.